Seeing Shelley Plain

Seeing Shelley Plain

by

Robert A. Wilson

Oak Knoll Press
New Castle, Delaware
2001

First Edition
Published by **Oak Knoll Press**
310 Delaware Street, New Castle, Delaware, USA

ISBN: 1-58456-050-9

Title: Seeing Shelley Plain
Author: Robert A. Wilson
Typographer: Angela Werner of Michael Höhne Design
Cover Design: Michael Höhne
Publishing Director: J. Lewis von Hoelle

Library of Congress Cataloging-in-Publication Data

Wilson, Robert A. (Robert Alfred), 1922–
    Seeing Shelley plain : memories of New York's legendary Phoenix Book Shop /
Robert A. Wilson.
        p. cm.
    Includes bibliographical references and index.
    ISBN 1-58456-050-9
    1. Phoenix Book Shop. 2. Bookstores--New York (State)--New York--
History--20th century. 3. Wilson, Robert A. (Robert Alfred), 1922–
4. Booksellers and bookselling--New York (State)--New York--Biography.
5. Publishers and publishing--New York (State)--New York--Biography.
6. Authors, American--20th century--Biography. 7. New York (N.Y.)--
Intellectual life--20th century. I. Title

Z473.P477 W55 2001
381'.45002'09747--dc21
                                                                    00-069227

Printed in the United States of America on 60# archival, acid-free paper meeting the
requirements of the American standard for Permanence for Printed Library Materials.

Table of Contents

For

Marshall Clements

who reawakened my interest
in books and poetry,
and most importantly,
took me to the
Phoenix Book Shop
for the very first time

Acknowledgments

Thanks are due to James Grauerholz for permission to quote the inscription by William Burroughs; to Andreas Brown of the Gotham Book Mart for permission to print the letter from and the photograph of Frances Steloff; and to Dr. Donald Gallup and to Alan Clodd for providing, transatlantically, the stanza from Robert Browning's poem "Memorabilia".

My only hope is that this book will not disappoint the many people who have constantly encouraged me to record my memories, particularly Marshall Clements, Dr. Donald Gallup, Dr. Jack Hagstrom, Jim Perrizo, and Mark Mason. Finally I must acknowledge my indebtedness to my good friend Ken Doubrava, who patiently listened to these anecdotes innumerable times, and Mary Hallwachs, whose keen eye in correcting the original manuscript for typos and errors is truly remarkable. But even more important is her unique sense of cadence and rhythm, pointing out the stylistic awkwardnesses and tiresome repetitions. Without their unflagging help, this account might never have come to life.

OTHER WORKS BY ROBERT A. WILSON

A Bibliography of Gregory Corso, 1966

A Bibliography of Denise Levertov, 1972

Gertrude Stein: A Bibliography, 1974

Gertrude Stein: A Bibliography (Revised), 1994

Modern Book Collecting, 1980

Modern Book Collecting, Second (corrected) Edition, 1986

Preface

   This memoir has been worked on sporadically ever since the closing of the Phoenix in 1988. But I must admit that for several years many other things occupied my attention while I continued answering inquiries about progress with a statement that was barely truthful—"I'm working on it,"—when actually I hadn't done much more than revise some of the Christmas pamphlets.

   Then along came the young dealer from New Hampshire, John LeBow, who conceived the idea of publishing a *festschrift* in honor of the Phoenix. In addition to tributes by several of the major poets who had frequented the Phoenix, he wanted something from me, so I gave him the first chapter of this memoir. When *The Phoenix Book Shop: a Nest of Memories* was published in 1997, I was very pleasantly surprised by the great interest shown in it.

   I decided then and there to get to work in earnest on the memoir and, for better or worse, here is the result.

Part One

The Memoirs

I

Getting Started

"Sell me a book tonight, Larry. You haven't sold me a book in weeks."

"Why don't you buy all of them?"

"Okay, how much?"

With that bantering exchange in 1959 began the steps which ultimately led me to becoming the fifth in the apostolic succession of owners of
the Phoenix Book Shop in Greenwich Village. Larry Wallrich, the fourth
owner, had run the shop for some six years, with the part-time help of his
wife Ruby. Occasionally the poet Diane di Prima, then just beginning her
literary career, would also help out. When Larry replied to my query about
price he named a precise figure, one that he had obviously thought about,
not just an off-hand reply to a jest.

"You're serious, aren't you?" I replied.

"Yes, aren't you?"

"Well I wasn't, but I could be." With that he got up from his desk and
went to the front door, locking it and turning off the window lights.
Obviously Larry was very serious. He proceeded to explain that he wanted
to move his wife and child to Europe, since he did not want his kids growing up on the streets of New York. At that time I was employed as the office
manager of a cuckoo clock factory, and while the salary was adequate to my
needs, even allowing for the occasional purchase of a book for my then
beginning Gertrude Stein collection, I had reached a dead end. There was no
further advancement possible, and the best I could look forward to was a

yearly modest salary increase to keep pace with the inflation that was just then beginning. I was ripe for a change.

However there was one major obstacle: within a matter of weeks I was escorting my parents on their first and only grand tour of Europe. This had been planned for nearly two years, with reservations made and plane tickets paid for. Obviously it would be impossible to delay our departure. I couldn't possibly undertake the transfer of the shop to me until I returned three months later at the beginning of the summer.

Don't worry," Larry said, "We can wait until you get back." I suggested that we draw up an agreement and that I make a binding down payment, but Larry said it wasn't necessary and that we had a gentlemen's agreement. He wouldn't sell it to anyone else during my absence.

As soon as possible after we returned from Europe I hurried down to 18 Cornelia Street, filled with excitement and expectations. Both of these feelings were dashed within minutes of my entering the shop. After a brief discussion of the trip, I asked Larry when we could begin the formal proceedings for me to purchase the shop.

"I can't sell it to you. The deal is off."

Shocked and stunned, I could only reply, "But Larry, you gave me your word you would wait for me to get back."

"I know I did and I'm not going to sell it to anyone else. It's a personal matter that I can't discuss with you right now. I can't sell it now at all. I'll let you know when it will be possible, but for now it simply cannot be done."

There was nothing to do but acquiesce and wait and hope. Finally, some months later, Larry did explain—his wife was pregnant. At the time I had returned they were awaiting medical confirmation. Now it was a matter of waiting for the birth of the child. Soon after his son was born, I raised the question again. This time I was told that it simply wasn't sage to move a newborn baby to a different climate, different water, and so on. We would have to wait until the child was somewhat older. I waited slightly over a year and again renewed my offer, only to be told that Ruby was once again pregnant.

"Will you stop it!" I blurted out.

So for the third time there was a delay. But finally, three years and two babies later, Larry was ready, I was ready and his wife was not pregnant. It all went smoothly, in the matter of a few weeks, most of the time being spent in my putting together the financing of the venture. Larry obviously needed full cash payment to transfer his now substantial family all the way to Europe, in fact to Majorca.

The price was eleven thousand dollars. Added to this were various closing fees and the lawyer's fee, so in effect I needed twelve thousand, which doesn't sound like much now, but in 1962 it was substantial. My salary, before deductions, was one hundred dollars a week, meaning, in essence, eighty dollars. To put that sum together I took what little I had in the bank, sold my share of the family farm to my cousin Bill, borrowed from my mother and a lady friend, Marie Hesse, and finally got a loan under the GI Bill of Rights.

I gave notice at the cuckoo clock factory and spent the week up to the final day sitting in with Larry to learn the ropes and become familiar with whatever might be in process at the time of the transfer. This had been set for the close of business at the end of the last week in March, 1962.

In those days the shop closed at 11 p.m., having opened at 3 p.m., ordinary business hours for Greenwich Village. A couple of hours before the appointed time Larry decided not to wait any longer and suggested we do it at once. Since this transfer was to take place well after normal business hours, our respective attorneys had drawn up the papers in such a manner that all we had to do was go to a notary, sign the deed, and hand over to Larry the check in payment, along with, rightfully, the cash proceeds for the day. So we locked the door and went around the corner to a Sixth Avenue liquor store ,the owner of which also functioned as a notary. We accomplished the transaction in short order. Larry handed me the keys, congratulating me as he did so. He disappeared almost before I realized that in a cheap booze emporium at 9:30 at night I had at last embarked on my life's true work. I went back to 18 Cornelia Street and for the first time turned the key in the lock of the Phoenix Book Shop.

I had taken on a good bit of responsibility at a late date in my life: after all, I would be forty within a week. To begin with, I had practically no cash after putting together the purchase money. Not only did I have no further resources, I was in hock up to my neck, with no less than three separate loans to pay off. Added to this was the fact that I had no real hands-on business experience. My six years as office manager at the cuckoo clock factory had in actuality entailed little more than seeing that invoices were sent out, ordering office supplies on time, and answering the telephone. On top of this, in the book collecting field my knowledge and expertise was limited to the four authors whom I had collected in a serious manner: Mencken, Hemingway, Stein and Marianne Moore. I could also add a smidgen of knowledge about Ezra Pound, at that time rather low in the esteem of collectors (to say nothing of the U.S. Government).

This knowledge had been gained by going book hunting with my friend Marshall Clements, who had introduced me to the work of Ezra Pound (among many other diverse pleasures.) In other words, I was "run-

Entrance to The Phoenix, 18 Cornelia Street

ning scared." But running scared seemed to me preferable to working in a small corporate office in an atmosphere I had come increasingly to dislike— so much so that during my last year there I had tried to get fired in order to qualify for unemployment insurance while I sought other work. But the ploy backfired. The owners finally realized that I was desperately unhappy, and instead of firing me they gave me a substantial raise. Welcome as this was, it did nothing to remove my basic dislike of what I was doing. Here at the bookshop I was at least my own boss, doing something I loved. After the euphoria of the weekend had worn off, I opened the door at 18 Cornelia that first morning in April 1962 as one who could not help thinking that the old adage "life begins at forty" was really true.

That Monday turned out to be very chilly, so when I entered the shop I quickly found out what the first thing to do should be: provide some heat. The shop was located on the street floor of a building more than a century old, and while heat had been installed for the apartments on the floors above, there was none in the shop. The only source of warmth there was from a classic pot-bellied stove in the middle of the store, surmounted by a series of stovepipes that took as many turns and bends as a Rube Goldberg contraption. Beside it I found a scuttle with some coal in it, (later I found a large bin of coal in the back room) and set about building a fire at once. Fortunately this was a skill I had learned in my wartime service in the infantry. Soon the stove was glowing cherry red, and had to be dampened down to lessen the prodigious amount of heat it was throwing off.

Scarcely had I gotten the fire going when I heard the door being pushed open, and to my astonishment there stood Frances Steloff, proprietor of the legendary Gotham Book Mart, and at that time indisputably the most famous book seller in the entire world. I had been a customer of hers long before I had ever dreamed of owning my own shop. In fact, I had bought my first rare book (Hemingway's *God Rest Ye, Merry Gentlemen*) from her in 1943 when I was stationed on Long Island during my military service in W.W. II. I was even more stunned when she said on entering, "I heard about your buying the Phoenix and I want to be your first customer."

To this day I have never found out how she knew exactly when the transfer was to become effective; after all, it had been in the works, off and on, for three years. And there had been no public notice. But there she was, taking precious time out from her own shop to give a boost to a potential competitor. I'll never forget the graciousness of that gesture. Alas, I cannot remember what it was she purchased, but I do remember clearly her refusal to take the customary dealer's discount which I offered her. "No," she said, "Not on your first sale."

After Frances left I began my first day, opening the mail and trying to fill a couple of orders that came in from a catalog that Larry had issued several weeks before. This took place late in the afternoon, since the official opening time was 3 p.m., not at all unusual in Greenwich Village in those halcyon, crime-free days. In fact, most of my neighboring business establishments opened at 4. Technically we closed at 11 p.m., but this was rarely strictly observed, even though I had an hour's subway ride, once the train came along, to my apartment at the upper end of Manhattan, just south of the George Washington Bridge.

With no street crime to fear, the biggest influx of customers was generally around 8 p.m., after people had finished their dinners and came out for a stroll. This meant that my own supper had to be eaten in the shop, between customer visits, after I had prepared it on a two-burner gas stove in the back room. This resulted at least once in another friendly gesture. The

With Frances Steloff at the Gotham Book Mart

sink was piled up one night with dirty dishes when Peter Orlovsky and Allen Ginsberg came in, and Peter, ever the neatness freak, asked why things were so messy. I explained to him that there had been so many customers that night that I hadn't yet had an opportunity to do any washing up. Then another customer came in, and after I had waited on him, I was astonished to see Peter and Allen washing the dishes for me, and Peter even going on to do some more general tidying up.

Heady as it was to be my own boss and in a business that seemed more like play than work, it soon became painfully apparent that the day-to-day business wasn't sufficient to pay the rent, let alone start paying off the three loans that had been necessary to supplement my own funds for the purchase of the Phoenix. I had also to consider the fact that I had to subsist personally. The only possible solution was to issue a catalog. Wallrich had already started doing this before the beginning of our protracted negotiations. In fact, I had upbraided him when I received a catalog numbered "50." I had been a customer for a couple of years and had never before received such a mailing. He grinned and said that it was his first catalog.

"Well, why is it number 50 then?" I countered.

"I didn't want to look like a beginner by calling it number 1," was his reply, with the grin turning into a loud chuckle. Larry's last catalog had been number 59, so I started on number 60.

Actually it wasn't the first catalog I had issued. Before my purchase of the shop, during the seemingly endless wait, I had issued two very slight twelve-page catalogs run off surreptitiously at the cuckoo clock factory to dispose of material I had bought over the years in the belief that they were more valuable than the modest price they bore in the Fourth Avenue shops. These catalogs were rather grandly entitled *A Modest Miscellany of Fine Firsts and Other Oddments* and *A Second Selection of Prime Printings for Discriminating Devotees.* Obviously I am very fond of alliteration. Whatever the case may be, I'm afraid the catalog titles were far more lofty than any of the items I had to offer, with possibly a couple of exceptions.

It may be instructive to read what the price scale was in 1959-1960. How about John Berryman's first book, *Poems,* in the New Directions series known as The Poet of the Month for $2.75? Or a Cummington Press imprint for $2.00? Or maybe you'd like *The Grapes of Wrath* in a mint dust jacket for $5.00? Luckily, the highest priced item did not sell—an inscribed copy of President Kennedy's *Profiles in Courage,* priced at $35.00. I still have it, along with books inscribed to me by two other presidents, Dwight D. Eisenhower and Harry S Truman. I wasn't quite as lucky with the star item of the second catalog, for some hawk-eyed customer snapped up a Civil War history with a nice chatty inscription by F. Scott Fitzgerald for $12.50. I was quite thrilled to make such a handsome profit, for I had found it on a sidewalk stand for fifty cents.

One seemingly minor decision concerning one of the books in that first catalog proved to be a far-reaching, crucial one for the eventual success of the Phoenix. An assistant librarian at the Henry Huntington Library and Art Gallery in California had ordered for himself one of the *Best Short Story* anthologies containing an early Hemingway short story. I had described it as fine, but when I went to wrap it for shipment I noticed a small worm-hole in the spine that I had not seen previously. I went ahead and shipped it, but cut the price in half. This proved to be the correct decision, for there began a friendship which has lasted to this day. A couple of years later this librarian made a career move and transferred to the prestigious Lilly Library at Indiana University at Bloomington, whose collection of the moderns was just beginning. He proved in the years ahead to be the Phoenix's most loyal and supportive customer. Now that the Phoenix is no longer in existence, its archive is housed there.

Included in the equipment that I had inherited with the shop was a mimeograph machine which I thought I could operate if I could figure out the technicalities of typing the stencils so that the pagination would work out correctly. Larry's catalogs consisted of forty pages, which meant that two pages were typed on each stencil. By taking one of those catalogs apart I learned that page one was conjugate with page forty. So, by typing page one on the right half of the long stencil, and alternating on each succeeding one until I got to page forty, it would work out properly when the sheets were run off and folded in half. It took me nearly six weeks to type them, having to do it whenever time permitted during the regular business of the shop. Finally I was able to put out catalog 60.

In selecting the contents for my first Phoenix catalog, I followed Larry's model and offered selections from the various categories of the stock—fiction, poetry, literary criticism, periodicals, art books, and a small batch of first editions. I had decided right from the beginning that I wanted to work off all this stock so that I could concentrate on first editions, although I had no clear idea just where they would come from after I had run through most of my minuscule holdings in that area. Sources were unknown to me other than the obvious combing of the Fourth Avenue shops for the occasional sleeper.

One of the first questions I had asked Larry during our negotiations was for a list of his sources. He declined to name them, but guaranteed that they would show up. This wasn't very comforting, but obviously there was nothing I could do about it except wait and see. However as he had said, people did start coming in offering books for sale—a lot of them directly from the younger group of authors, chronically in need of cash.

Looking now at that first of my Phoenix catalogs, I am astounded at how much really significant material was in it; a two-page typed letter by William Burroughs with a holographic postscript by Allen Ginsberg; a sixteen-page typed poem by Allen with manuscript revisions; four drawings for a proposed but never executed comic strip by Jack Kerouac; three paintings by Kenneth Patchen; as well as letters and manuscripts by Michael McClure and Gregory Corso. I did not realize it at the time, but the direction that the Phoenix would take was clearly spelled out in the last two pages of that catalog where those items appeared. The catalog sold better than I had hoped, and I realized that the regular issuance of catalogs would keep the Phoenix afloat while the loans were gradually paid off.

The Phoenix Catalogs

The mailing list which came with the shop consisted of approximately fifteen hundred names and addresses, about half of which seemed to be comprised of every university library in the entire United States. Although only a small handful of these ever ordered, I kept on sending them catalogs despite occasional thoughts of saving on the ever-increasing postage bills by eliminating most of them. Luckily I refrained from doing so. After about two years of catalogs, I decided to issue what I privately called a "house-cleaning" catalog. In other words, if I listed an author, I put in absolutely everything in the shop by or about him, including periodical appearances. Wallrich had left me an enormous stock of these, including large quantities of *Poetry Magazine,* some of which were the second copyright copies, acquired when the Library of Congress, to gain much needed space, decided to release its duplicate copies. Shortly after this catalog was in the mail, I received an order from a university that had never ordered anything before. The more I looked at it, the more amazed I became. It was a huge order for several hundred items. After I spent the better part of that night pulling the books off the shelf and starting to invoice the order, something that had eluded me suddenly became apparent. If they ordered a title by an author, they ordered absolutely everything by him in the catalog. Obviously this was a university beginning an in-depth collection of English and American literature of the twentieth century, down to magazine appearances, something that virtually no other university that I knew of was doing. It took nearly a week to wrap and pack the books and lug the heavy cartons to the post office. After this was all done, I wrote to the librarian who had signed the order and told him I could provide much more material, asking if he would like to receive quotations before such items appeared in a catalog. The reply that came back immediately was what enabled the Phoenix to get out of the red and pay off the loans.

This order was from the University of Nevada at Reno, and just as I surmised, they were beginning a collection, thanks to a substantial grant by the state legislature, to form a reference collection of modern literature based on bibliographic completeness. They sent me their author list, adding that they were particularly pleased to find a source for secondary material, especially magazines. When they had started their collection they were acquainted with several dealers who could supply the primary titles, but until receiving my catalog they were worried about being able to add anthologies and periodicals to their holdings.

With their author list in hand, I spent the next few months combing the shop and sending them lists from which they invariably bought everything I had to offer. It was a dream situation, both clearing out old stock, a lot of it inherited from Larry, and also bringing in a hefty income. In fact, in that first year this university provided one-third of the year's entire business.

In all, starting with catalog number 60, we were to issue some one hundred and fifty-seven catalogs. usually four a year but occasionally five. Once the general stock had been disposed of, these catalogs consisted almost exclusively of first editions and related items such as manuscripts, letters, autographs, photographs, periodicals and, of course, newly published volumes of poetry. A run-through of the great items that were sold via the U.S. mails would become tedious and boring, but a few words should be said of the more unusual catalogs. Twice we had accumulated enough material to issue an all-Gertrude Stein catalog, and once we acquired a mammoth Henry Miller collection which filled an entire catalog. Miller heard about this and wrote asking for some copies of it, adding that he knew the location of the shop very well, as at one period in his early years he had been a bartender in a saloon located nearby. And one time we had simultaneously collections of H. Rider Haggard and John Addington Symonds, allowing us to issue our *Two Victorians* catalog, complete with an appropriately ornate Victorian Gothic design on the cover.

Several times we had catalogs devoted exclusively to periodicals. For the first of these I asked Marianne Moore, as the former editor of one of the country's most distinguished literary journals, *The Dial,* to write an introduction. She graciously assented and provided a short statement which I used on the front cover. It read, "I cherish the personal book-shop. What an Elysium is a shop of which the owner reads some of the items he sells! One double-owns anything which he sells."

I was rather amused a few weeks later to receive a catalog from our neighbor, the Eighth Street Bookshop, who, not wanting to be outdone, had also obtained a similar quote from Miss Moore. And once, thanks to an acquisition of large collections, we had an all-Black catalog, and also an all-Irish catalog. For the latter we were unable to resist the temptation to change the ink in our mimeograph machine to green.

With catalog ninety-eight we began to improve the appearance of our straightforward, no-nonsense approach using mimeographed pages and covers. The invention of electronic stencils allowed us to have illustrated covers. Usually we employed old engravings or cuts from design books. Once we had an artist draw an original design for us, which caused some artistic jealousy. One of the shop's regular customers was a close friend of Marshall's, the painter Robert de Niro, whose legitimate fame as a painter has been eclipsed by that of his actor son. At any rate, one night Marshall asked De Niro to draw a cover design for us, which he quite willingly did on the spot. As it happened, the painter Nell Blaine was not only a good friend, but also a regular purchaser from our catalogs. When she received her copy with the De Niro cover drawing, she was upset and telephoned immediately to demand why she had never been asked to do a cover. Marshall explained, "Nell, we can't afford to pay for cover art."

This did not matter, apparently. Famous as she was, Nell felt that she needed to appear on one of our covers, and thereupon set out to do a superb India ink drawing for free (as well as letting me keep the original.) She did demand that we have it properly printed and not reproduced by electronic stencil. Many years later, in 1980, when Knopf-Random House commissioned her to design the cover for my *Modern Book Collecting,* I was both surprised and pleased to see that she had reworked the black and white illustration into a full color painting.

One further catalog should be mentioned. Being congenitally unable to throw away any printed matter, I had accumulated an enormous quantity of ephemera: such items as publicity brochures with blurbs by well-known writers, posters for poets' readings, publicity photos, etc. Many collectors like such material, but it was hardly economical to take up valuable catalog space for items you couldn't price higher than a couple of dollars. So one time I decided to list all this stuff, but run off only one hundred copies of the catalog to send to those who would be genuinely interested, rather than have the postage expense for the usual fifteen hundred names on the list.

Drawing by painter Robert DeNiro for Phoenix Catalog #99

Since I did not want there to be a break in the numerical sequence, which would inevitably have generated a lot of inquiries plus explanations on my part, I made this one a half-number—Catalog 105 1/2. It was extremely successful. but while typing it out, I got carried away and decided to have a bit of private fun by listing two nonexistent items just to see if anyone would catch on to the hoax. I listed a "very worn telephone directory for the town of Rapallo in Italy for the year 1937," describing it as lacking its cover, and the pages well-worn and dog-eared, but listing Ezra Pound's phone num-

Design by Nell Blaine for Catalog #100

ber, which I also invented. The other item I described was a framed butter-fly, "genus unknown as the label has fallen off the box," but inscribed "Given to me by Prof. Nabokov during my senior year." To my great delight I received several orders for both items, and half of them from university libraries. I always replied that, regrettably, they had already been sold. One of my customers, to whom I confided the secret, was so amused that he offered to go halves on the expense of putting out an entire such catalog. Fetching as the idea was, I simply could not afford to spare the time it would have taken.

Another thing that amused me greatly was the fact that not one, but two poets who were also engaged in publishing decided to issue parodies of the Phoenix catalogs. The first was the irrepressible Ed Sanders, publisher of the ground-breaking *FUCK YOU! a magazine of the arts.* He was so amused by the entire specialized lingo of the first edition world that he issued a catalog sati-rizing it all, as well as offering a wide variety of sometimes spurious but legit-imate-sounding items from the Beat world. He also bestowed on me a nick-name (which lasts until this day) when he listed a catalog entry under "WILSON, (Robert)—No we're not selling Bob Wilson, but seven of his recent catalogs. Watch Evil Wilson as he manipulates the rare book market." I took it in good grace and was truly flattered as well as amused. It wasn't long before I started receiving mail and phone calls addressed to "Evil" Wilson.

The other parody stemmed from Robert Bly's Ox Head Press, which had been publishing his circle of poet-friends. In 1979 three of them wrote parodies of the older poets such as Frost, Stevens and Williams, among oth-ers. The back cover of this pamphlet was what was purported to be an ad from the "Pheenix (sic) Book Shop" with spurious items that were even more outlandish than those of Ed Sanders. Didn't someone say "Imitation is the sincerest form of flattery."?

III

Some Important Finds

The year 1965 saw the start of another regular feature—periodic trips to London, usually every other year, on book-buying expeditions. The first one enabled me to make personal contacts with all the British dealers in the moderns, resulting in most cases in warm, personal friendships, as well as being offered choice items. The highlight in this category was the original working manuscript of Dylan Thomas' masterpiece *Under Milk Wood.* Its acquisition and delivery to a major institution is a saga in itself. It started when the new director of the Rosenbach Museum in Philadelphia wanted to bring the Museum's holdings and area of interest further into the twentieth century.

Its founder, Dr. Rosenbach, had not admitted anyone subsequent to James Joyce into the truly fabulous collection. In fact, when he purchased the manuscript of *Ulysses* at the sale of John Quinn's library it represented at that time a considerable departure from his preoccupation with previous centuries. The new director had had some discussions with the trustees, and they had decided that perhaps Dylan Thomas was probably worthy of inclusion, but it was felt that all the important manuscripts had already been irretrievably acquired by rival institutions. For some reason still unknown to me, I suggested that there must be something "still out there," and that I would be on the lookout for it. To this day I have no idea why such an unlikely possibility occurred to me. Within a few weeks, the miracle happened.

One of the best-known British dealers was in New York, and as always paid me a visit. During the course of the evening, he casually inquired if I would be interested in purchasing the handwritten manuscript of *Under*

Milk Wood. Trying not to let my excitement show too much, I said I probably would be, but asked if I might have an option for two weeks. The dealer was rather startled and probably a bit disgruntled by my response, since I suspect he had been boasting rather than genuinely offering the manuscript for sale. But now he could hardly back out. However he did say that he could not allow me to offer it around for sale. I replied I had no intention of doing that, but merely wanted to confirm the sale with my customer. I telephoned the Rosenbach immediately, and the director soon secured the approval of his board of trustees for the purchase.

As soon as I could book a plane seat, I flew off to London to bring the treasure back by hand, not wanting to trust it to the international mails, especially as this was mid-December. I took the precaution of sending an advance deposit, although the dealer said that of course this was not necessary. When I landed at Heathrow Airport, the dealer had very kindly arranged to fetch me by car, and as we drove into London he laughingly told me that there had been a sort of cloak-and-dagger aspect to the transaction. It seemed that somehow the representative of an American university, famous for its bottomless pockets as well as its omnivorous snatching up of anything of importance, had arrived in London and had been to their shop just an hour earlier, and had even resorted to offering a higher price than that which had been agreed upon with me. The firm of Bertram Rota, Ltd., was quite honorable in the best traditions of the trade, and could honestly say to Mr. F. that the manuscript had already been sold, and that he was too late. I silently breathed a sigh of relief that I had paid the advance, even though that, too, would not have made any difference in Rota's reply. I could bring the Thomas crown jewel back in triumph, although not without a struggle with the United States Customs Service.

There had already been some trouble in getting it aboard the plane as carry-on luggage. Each page of the manuscript had been mounted on large archival boards, and the entire thing then enclosed in a large leather case. It turned out to be too wide to fit in the overhead bins, and too long to fit under my seat. A very friendly stewardess solved the problem by changing my seat to one by the emergency exit, where the extra space permitted me to wedge it under my seat, just barely.

Once we had landed in New York I proceeded through the normal customs check. The official in charge cared nothing about the manuscript but was intent on assessing duty on the leather case. The date was December 24th, and he said that it would have to remain in customs over the holiday. I had no intention of allowing this and asked him why it was necessary. I was told that it would have to be inspected by the chief of the customs service, and that it would take a long time. I looked at my watch and saw that it was just a bit past noon. So I said, "Well, we still have at least five hours. Let's get started."

Although annoyed at this, he had no choice but to call his superior, who was in another building. Apparently the chief told him to send the item along. I started to pick it up and go with the guard, but was told I couldn't touch it. He would have to carry it. With a mixture of anxiety and amusement, I dutifully trotted along side. The chief inspector seemed to be a pleasant man, and asked me what the problem was. I explained that I was trying to bring in a manuscript by a famous poet, but the officer on duty felt that the leather case was dutiable and would have to be appraised for the assessment of charges. The chief asked to look at it. I hesitated, thinking that if I couldn't carry it, I wouldn't be allowed to unwrap it, but I was instructed to do so. When I had it all unwrapped, he looked at it briefly and said to the guard that it was okay, no duty applicable. With a sigh of relief I started re-wrapping, and thanked him. As I got to the door, he called out, "I hope you make a lot of money when you publish it."

I went home to Baltimore for Christmas, lugging the manuscript along, as I was to deliver it to the museum in Philadelphia on my way back to New York a couple of days later. My family was astounded to see it, and felt that we should celebrate by listening to the recording of Thomas reading *A Child's Christmas in Wales.* Two days later I delivered it to the happy librarian. Although I never found out, I always hoped that the first person he showed it to was the member of the board of directors who had said that nothing of importance remained to be found.

Other important manuscripts came our way as well: Auden's Pulitzer Prize-winning *The Age of Anxiety;* the early play written jointly by Auden and Isherwood, *The Ascent of F6* (discovered in a tiny Alpine hamlet in the Tyrol); Conrad Aiken's *The Blue Voyage,* generally regarded as his best novel; Henry Miller's *Quiet Days in Clichy;* and lastly and most importantly, the long-lost manuscript of Faulkner's first novel *Soldier's Pay,* which will be discussed in a later chapter.

The book-buying trips, while primarily taken to comb the British shops, also provided me with the opportunity of bringing back foreign translations of collected American authors. Several private collectors as well as a couple of university libraries collected such. After spending two weeks in London, I generally took a personal vacation and visited, ultimately, virtually all of the European capitals, thus finding many translations, copies of which seldom, if ever, appeared in the U.S. It was always surprising to see which authors managed to be published abroad. It surprised me to find that more translations of American authors were published in Denmark than in all the other European countries put together. This was doubly surprising to me in that it was obvious that more Danes spoke English than did the natives of any other continental country. It would seem that those interested could probably read the works in the original. Whatever the reason, I was always able to find large quantities of translations to ship home. And they always sold out immediately.

IV

Branching Out

I t was just about this time in the late 60s that another regular feature got started—that of supplying various institutions with newly published material, usually poetry, although two university libraries wanted fiction by a select list of authors as well as poetry. It started with Indiana University's Lilly Library asking me to supply such. This, along with a similar but slightly different list (including British authors also), from the University of Nevada got the program going. Somehow various other institutional libraries that were interested in the emerging moderns wanted a similar standing order arrangement for all new poetry that I deemed worthy of their attention.

I don't know why they started coming to me, but I suppose one librarian mentioned it to another; after all, they form a relatively tiny group. At its height, the standing order service was being employed by fourteen libraries. This allowed me to purchase a dozen or more of each new issue. I'm afraid that sometimes I probably supplied some poetry offerings that wouldn't really stand up to close reading or the inevitable test of time. But I had been given free rein, and it seemed to me better to err on the side of all-inclusiveness than run the risk of failing to recognize some budding new talent. How easy it would be to do this is pointed out in the case of Ezra Pound. His first two books, *A Lume Spento* and *A Quinzaine for This Yule,* while now being two of the rarest of twentieth-century poetry titles, contain nothing that would give any hint of Pound's eventual greatness. In fact, years later he himself termed them "stale cream puffs." I have often reflected that had I been around at that time and had I read those first two books, I would

have given up on Pound, and would not have bought anything more—
thereby missing his third book *Personae,* which is still one of the benchmark
volumes of twentieth-century verse.

And of course the struggling young would-be poets soon learned that
I would purchase a dozen copies of whatever they brought in, often produced by mimeograph. More often than not, such a sale meant the difference between the poet's going hungry that night or not.

At any rate, not a single one of the institutions ever complained about
anything I sent them. But, sorry to say, by the late 70s the heady days of fat
budgets and government subsidies began to wane as Republican congresses
kept hacking away at federal endowments until all such funding disappeared
totally under the Reagan regime. One by one, these university libraries were
forced to limit their spending on new issue material drastically, or, in many
cases, cease their programs altogether. By the time the 80s came in, only two
of the original libraries were still actively buying, and even they had been
forced to eliminate many names from their lists. Whether or not there is any
correlation between the two, it also seemed to me that the virtual renaissance
of American poetry had just about run its course, and very few new voices
with much sign of promise were appearing.

But while things were going strong, and orders increasing along with
the shop's reputation as the only place in town where all new poetry could
be found, it became very clear to me that I could no longer run the shop
single-handedly. So the Phoenix soon had its first employee—a packing boy.
In the first two years I could have used help, but the income was so minimal
that I took no salary on a fixed basis. I simply paid for my basic personal
expenses—rent, food, insurance, and a bit of pocket money—out of the
shop's check book. At the end of the month the accountant would add these
up and declare that sum my "salary." Now, with the added revenue, I was
drawing a regular, fixed, if still modest salary, with enough left over to afford
a part-time packer.

Several came and went, including the colorful Larry Ree, who went
on to fame, if not fortune, as the founder and star of the Trocadera Gloxinia
ballet troupe, an all-male group performing, among other ballets, *Swan
Lake,* in such exalted venues as the Edinburgh Festival. But at last a close
friend recommended a young man recently married, who needed some part-
time work to supplement the salary from his day job. This was convenient

for both of us, due to the late hours the shop was open. Thus it was that Freddie Martinez came to work at the Phoenix, and stayed for a dozen years until he finally quit because he wanted to spend more time with his growing children. I was very sorry to see him leave, but understood completely why he felt he had to quit. From then on, until the closing of the shop, several packers worked for various periods of time, but none was as reliable and efficient as Freddie.

By the late 60s the shop's reputation both as a haven for new poetry and as an important source for modern first editions had begun to spread world wide, and it became clear that it could not grow further without some full-time assistance in addition to the packer. So during the last two decades of the shop's existence there was a series of four such employees. First there was my very close friend Marshall Clements, who was looking for a job after his then employer died. Since Marshall was the one who had reawakened my long dormant interest in literature, and had been the one who first introduced me to the work of Ezra Pound, Gertrude Stein and Michael McClure, I was more than delighted to have him as my assistant. At that time we were still keeping the 3 to 11 p.m. hours. Marshall preferred the usual business hours, so we agreed to open the shop early and he would leave at 5 or 6 p.m., giving us an overlap time together in the late afternoon. Shortly after he started at the Phoenix we made one more change. One of his previous colleagues went into medical practice on his own and wanted Marshall's services one day a week. So it was that our "late Wednesdays" came about, with Marshall arriving about the same time that I usually did in the afternoon, and staying until closing time. This meant that we shared dinner. One of our favorites was to get a large pizza from one of the neighboring Italian establishments around the corner on Bleecker Street, accompanied by a superb California wine with the charming double-dactylic name Inglenook Zinfandel, alas no longer bottled. About a year after Marshall had started, David Stivender, the Metropolitan Opera's chorus master came in. Although I describe David in the chapter on Louis Zukofsky, this is one part of his story that belongs here. Sometimes David wanted to come down after the Met's opera performance was over, and he would ask us to wait a few minutes longer to give him time to come down from Lincoln Center. After a couple of such episodes, we decided to close the Phoenix and then go to a neighborhood coffee shop where we could continue our discussions of books, literature, the opera, sex, whatever struck our fancy. Either Marshall or David coined an acronym for these evenings, the "WELLL"—the "Wednesday Evening Literary League." Yes, I know that I have written three "Ls." I leave it to the astute reader to decipher that third "L."

After some years, Marshall received a job offer he couldn't refuse, the proffered salary was not one that I could match, so with a great deal of sadness, Marshall left, *senza rancor,* as Mimi says in *La Boheme.*

Then another close friend, Kenneth Doubrava, who usually worked as an office temp, offered to fill in. But the rare book world was not his forte, and after two years I once again had to find a new assistant. Kenneth was succeeded by a young man who had often sold me first editions, and who was very knowledgeable in that field. All went well for a couple of years, but then he married, and started making demands that could not possibly be made without bankrupting the Phoenix. The result was his departure to set up a book business of his own. The less said about that the better, except to note that his venture did not succeed.

At first I was somewhat bitter about this turn of events, but in reality it was the proverbial blessing in disguise, for I was extremely lucky to gain the services of Dick Schaubeck, whom I had known for quite some time as co-publisher, with Frank Hallman, of handsome and superbly crafted limited editions by current authors. Dick worked diligently and flawlessly right up until the end of the Phoenix. Without him the best days of the Phoenix would not have been as happy and glorious as they were.

With competent full-time assistance, I was free to do more cataloging, and we were soon issuing five a year instead of the usual four. Luckily we were never at a loss for material, although naturally a lot of it consisted of newly published titles, or relatively inexpensive items. More often than not these titles were unobtainable from many other dealers, who felt that it was financially a losing proposition to catalog such items. This was one of the benefits of issuing no-nonsense mimeographed catalogs—we could afford to list these things. I always felt that while it was thrilling to offer a Faulkner manuscript or a letter by James Joyce, the elusive Beat pamphlet priced at five dollars was just as important. And such things helped build a following among young collectors who might otherwise have lost interest in collecting when there was nothing in a catalog they could afford.

Kenneth Doubrava and Robert Wilson at 18 Cornelia Street

V

The Phoenix Moves

O f course it was not always unalloyed fun. The Phoenix, like every other book store that has ever existed, suffered from occasional thievery. All bookstore owners dread the coming of winter, for bulky overcoats are the shoplifter's main tool. Sorry to say, my shop was no exception. It was not only small or thin volumes that disappeared. Once even a first edition of Gertrude Stein's magnum opus *The Making of Americans,* a hefty, large book roughly the size of the New York telephone directory disappeared from a shelf directly opposite my desk and at eye level.

Another depredation was not discovered until long after the book's actual disappearance. Some clever thief had removed a signed limited book by Erskine Caldwell from its fancy slipcase and had simply turned the case around so that the spine of the empty box faced outward. Only once was I ever able to recover a purloined book—Steinbeck's first, *The Cup of Gold.*

As luck would have it, I had just placed it on the shelf one evening. Shortly thereafter one of my regular scouts came in with some minor periodicals of little interest. I stepped into the back room briefly to turn down the fire under my dinner, returning to find the scout gone, as well as the Steinbeck title. No other person had been in the shop after I had placed it on the shelf, so it was a clear-cut case.

I immediately notified the AB, as *The Antiquarian Bookman* trade journal is familiarly referred to. Helping to recover stolen books is one of its many services to dealers. A brief notice appeared in the next issue, and the elegant Madison Avenue dealer Philip Duschnes telephoned me and asked if I could identify the copy. I replied that I could not; there were no identifying marks in this particular copy, but I could describe and name the person who had sold it to him. Thus the book came back to me, but alas, on other occasions I was not so lucky.

However, one learns to survive these thefts, no matter how irritating or financially serious they may be. Two other events were far more devastating. In one case it resulted in the destruction of a friendship and the loss of trust and respect for one of the major poets of the time, especially troubling as I had performed many services for him over the years. Poets are almost always impecunious, especially if they have an expensive addiction to support, as this Beat poet had. Nonetheless, it was his poetry that first led me to take an interest in the Beat movement, and despite it all, I still regard his poetry as the best work to have came out of that movement

I often bought books, manuscripts and letters from him, whatever he had to sell. Once he came in offering to sell me the holographic manuscript of a minor short pamphlet by Allen Ginsberg, explaining that he had asked Allen for money, but having no ready cash, Allen had given him the manuscript to sell in lieu of actual dollars. This was a well-known practice of Ginsberg's—writing out something that could be turned into cash. Often youths would come in with a couple of books inscribed by him along with

Allan Ginsberg and Robert Wilson, 1991

a note from Allen suggesting that they bring them to me and I would in all likelihood purchase them. I also knew that Allen had been helping support this particular poet, on and off, for several years. So I took his statement at face value and bought the manuscript for *The Iron Horse*, which I promptly sold to my most assiduous Ginsberg collector.

Some weeks later Allen discovered that this manuscript was missing and realized who had pilfered it from him. He telephoned and roundly berated me for having bought it. I was shocked and extremely upset, for I had been duped, never a pleasant sensation. Not too many months later

Jones Street Entrance

Allen phoned again to apologize for his anger, telling me he could hear the anguish in my voice. The last thing I wanted was to have my friendship with Ginsberg destroyed. I tried to recover the manuscript, but the customer to whom I had sold it was adamant in his refusal to part with it. Neither Allen not I wanted to endure the loss of time and the expense of a legal procedure to regain possession, so Allen graciously agreed to accept a Xerox copy of the manuscript so that his archive would not have a gap in it.

A couple of years later, another young man came in with a large number of letters written to Allen, along with some small pocket journals in Allen's handwriting. Although I knew that this person was at the time employed as a secretary to Allen, alarms went off at once. I bought the material but immediately got in touch with Allen, who came over and retrieved the lot, most of which he had not known was gone. Allen graciously offered to split the amount of money I had laid out, but having no actual cash at the time, gave me his IOU. Allen never sent me any money nor did I ever bring the subject up. As luck would have it, a couple of years later the vendor in question confessed his crime and actually made good by repaying me in installments.

But worse than the monetary losses was the trouble that arose out of an offer to sell me a few letters written by W.H. Auden to one of his protégés. I was busy at the moment that this one brought them in, so he agreed that he would leave them with me and come back another day. They were lying on my desk when in came the poet previously alluded to. When closing up that night, I looked for the Auden letters, but could not find them. They had disappeared. I didn't take much imagination to figure out how they had left the shop.

When the protégé returned, I told him what had happened and said that of course I would pay him for the letters. I named what I thought was a reasonable figure; even at the casual glance I had given them when they were handed to me I could see that they were of little importance, being mainly concerned with setting dates for meetings. Alas, the owner had a very exaggerated idea of their worth, and decided to sue me for their supposed value.

The letters turned up later in a major research library which had bought them from another dealer, so the suit was expanded to include both the library and the other dealer. Since the owner of the letters could not

Photo by Kate Simon

With William Burroughs and Victor Bokris

afford a lawyer, he had filed his suit in small claims court, which meets at night and hears as many cases as possible. It quite often happens that closing time arrives before all cases have been heard, so those remaining are carried over until the next month. We had to appear every month for five months before the case was actually adjudicated, the judge naming a sum virtually identical to what I had originally offered. Appeals are not allowed in this court, so the owner went away very angry.

What next transpired was a constant barrage of harassment that went on for years. This included non-stop collect phone calls, tying up our lines for hours; calls to my home very late at night; and Crazy Glue being poured into the lock on the shop's door, making entry impossible and requiring replacement by a locksmith. This continued until the last day of the Phoenix.

But as disturbing as these things were, much worse were the frequent floods at 18 Cornelia Street. The building was well over one hundred years old, and the plumbing was constantly giving way, usually in the middle of the night when the shop was closed. This meant that floods starting on the upper floors seeped down the walls, with the water creeping out onto the shelves, ruining all the books on them. Sometimes this wasn't apparent until a book was removed from the shelf and the damage discovered. After this had happened five times, I decided that no matter what the increase in rent I would have to pay, I simply could not stay there any longer and run the risk of once more losing major portions of our inventory. I started looking for a new location. This was not easy, for I needed a place where I could afford the rent, and one that was also not too far from the original location, so that we would not lose our regular customers.

As luck would have it, one day while returning from the post office, Kenneth saw a "For Rent" sign on a newly renovated building just one block further west, at 22 Jones Street. After some waiting while another prospective tenant failed to take up his option on the space, we moved in 1975. This new space had a great many advantages. We weren't likely to be flooded out, there was much more space, and it also had heat. No longer would we have to build a fire every morning. And perhaps best of all, it was flooded with light through the floor-to-ceiling plate glass windows. Kenneth helped this move to go smoothly in many ways. He built new shelves and installed the ceiling light fixtures while I tried to keep the day-to-day and the mail-order business going as much as possible while superintending the packing up of the stock. The entire transition took us less than a month, with no major interruption to the flow of business. Of course as soon as we were settled we gave a housewarming party. Frances Steloff came, once again giving her blessing to what had now become a real competitor; an extremely gracious, not-to-be-forgotten gesture.

With the increase in available shelf space the size of the inventory grew. Now instead of having a small poetry section, a large part of the new area was devoted to current poetry. We tried to keep in stock every American poet of any distinction whatever (as well as some whose poetic talents were dubious, to say the kindest). This section was not very profitable, but now the much expanded first edition section produced enough revenue that we could afford to subsidize the poetry. In so doing we earned the affection of a great many poets. And since the craze in the book collecting world for having books signed by the authors had increased dramatically since I had first started, we would ask poets and authors to come in and sign copies of their newest works. We never charged a premium for these copies, and the authors were usually glad to cooperate since obviously this helped to increase sales.

One day three authors decided to show up the same afternoon, unbeknownst to each other. This resulted in a gathering unlike any in the Phoenix's long history. First there was Edward Albee, and shortly thereafter, while he was still signing, in came William Burroughs. Obviously they knew of each other but had never actually met, so I had the pleasure of introduc-

ing them. While they were both signing, in came Gregory Corso. While I
had met Burroughs on a couple of previous occasions, this was his first time
in the shop, so I asked him to write something in our guest book, which
Corso and Albee had signed some years before. It wasn't until much later
that day after they had all departed that I had the opportunity to read what
Burroughs had written. I was delighted to find that it was an on-the-spot
example of his famous "cut-up" technique. In this case, instead of rearrang-

ing snippets of printed prose, he had listened to the conversation going on amongst us all, and had blended phrases from each of us into one organic paragraph, the text of which is as follows:

> For Bob Wilson
> on the occasion of my first
> visit to the Phoenix Book Store
> messages are unscrambled from
> the Electronic Revolution
> Gregory won $5 on the altitude
> of holy faith. It will go
> for a good purpose. Why
> cant a human being take
> his words out and wash
> them? You could but it
> would hardly be worth
> while.
> William S. Burroughs
> breathed his third and
> last wish

VI

Never A Dull Moment

One of the chief pleasures in running the Phoenix was the opportunity it gave me to meet many of my literary idols, as well as providing occasional visits from celebrities in other disciplines. Movie and television stars seldom came in, although there were a few. John Larroquette surprised me by turning out to be a very knowledgeable and serious collector of the works of John Beckett. He was a totally different person from the one I had become familiar with in his long-running television sit-com Night Court. Shelley Winters once appeared in the first shop, ostensibly looking for old maps, but insisting on knowing what was in a great number of wrapped parcels on the highest shelves. She wasn't satisfied with my reply that they were merely copies of the Parisian literary magazine *Locus Solus,* and insisted that I haul one down and unwrap it for her. Lord knows what she was hoping to discover.

Once I was treated to the thrilling voice of Richard Burton, although I cannot remember what it was that he was looking for. And one other time I was titillated by thinking that I had discovered a secret passion of Keir Dullea's when he came in looking for books on sadism. Some time later my overactive imagination got its comeuppance when I learned that he was starring in a film biography of the Marquis de Sade!

A constant visitor from the world of drama was Edward Albee. He was very friendly and an engaging conversationalist, but very shy of the public. We would stay indefinitely chatting amiably and wittily, but as soon as a customer came in he would quickly depart without another word. Once I had a one-act play of mine produced in the Village at an off-Broadway theater, a repertory theater whose program changed every week. Albee asked how it had gone. In reply I told him how upset and annoyed I was when I went to the opening and discovered that the director had produced it as a comedy, whereas I had written an intensely serious play, or so I thought.

He said, "You shouldn't have let them," to which his companion chimed in, "Well, Edward, that's what happens to all your plays." Edward , like Victoria was not amused. Years later I realized that his companion that evening was Terrence McNally who, at that time, had not yet had a play produced.

Another infrequent visitor was a tall, elegant man with a mustache, always wearing a boutonniere, looking for all the world like a Parisian boulevardier. this turned out to be the humorist S.J. Perelman, who was always

Edward Albee

looking for his own out-of-print books. I never had any, but was careful to explain to him that the only reason for this was that they were in such demand that they always sold as soon as I put them on the shelf. Once I asked him to put something in the guest book, and in it he wrote, "We are both in a dying business, but what a way to go!"

Sometimes of necessity the encounters took place away from the shop, especially when authors had a large number of books to sell. One of the most colorful of such meetings began with a summons from Marya Zaturenska and her husband Horace Gregory. They lived in upper New Jersey, just north of the George Washington Bridge. At that time I did not own a car, so whenever a large quantity of books was involved, I asked my good friend Marie Hesse to drive me in her car. We found the house quite easily, it being located not far from Marie's residence in North Bergen. We were met at the door by Zaturenska herself, a large, portly woman, downright dumpy and plain, with the figure of a Russian peasant rather than that one might imagine of a Pulitzer Prize-winning poet. Nevertheless, she had the mind of a joyous Jesuit, is such a creature exists. Her husband was confined to a wheelchair, but still totally mentally alert.

After concluding the disappointingly meager book buying (as a book-buying expedition it had been a total failure, since all they wanted to part with was a quantity of recent review book,) we were treated to a brief tour of the house, (where I saw quite a lot of books I would have liked to purchase.) We were then invited to tea. This turned out to be madder than Lewis Carroll's classic Mad Hatter's tea party.

She kept warning us that setting a table was a science (her word) that had eluded her. After much backing and filling, with repeated trips to and from the kitchen, she finally announced that tea was ready. We sat down and she proceeded to pour. The spout of her teapot was broken, with the result that a considerable amount of the tea flooded the table rather than going into the cups. This was made even worse by the fact that she was looking at us instead of the cups as she poured, all the while talking at a great rate. In fact, she never stopped talking the entire time Marie and I were there. Finally all of our cups were more or less filled and we all settled down, only to realize that she had been correct about her inability to set a table. There were no spoons. Horace noticed this, and asked her to fetch some, which she did without interrupting her monologue.

Then a new crisis arose over what was the correct knife to employ in cutting the cheddar cheese. After two abortive attempts with a butter knife, a large kitchen knife was brought out and used more or less effectively. Zaturenska then proceeded to light her cigarette with a large wooden kitchen match. The head broke of, still aflame, and set fire to the tablecloth. In the ensuing slapping of the conflagration with her napkin, her elbow upset her teacup, flooding the table once again. This put out the fire, we all donated our individual napkins to stem the tide, and finally it was cleared away. During all this commotion her monologue continued unabated. It was filled with rather vicious barbs thrown at her literary peers, with remarks such as, "Allen Tate should have less loyalty and more discrimination."

She also claimed that Randall Jarrell was fond of writing anonymous obscene letters to women. She claimed that she had received several such, and, recognizing the handwriting, had threatened his editor with legal action, whereupon the letters ceased.

By then we were all ready for a second cup of tea, most of us having received very little in the first round. Marie handed her empty cup to our hostess, who returned it to me. I handed Zaturenska my cup and she kept it for herself. I said nothing, but gave Marie a meaningful look so that we could make our departure. On the way out I thanked our hostess for the tea and added that the next time I hoped there would be some better books for sale. She seemed miffed by this, saying, "But they are all excellent books." Apparently I had failed the test, for I was never invited back, much to my relief.

Unfortunately not all the encounters outside the shop were so humorous. some were rather serious, such as the time Charles Olson phoned me from the Sloan-Kettering Cancer Center in New York, on New Year's Eve, 1970, while a small party was in progress at my apartment. He had been transferred there from Boston, and I had already learned that he was dying. He asked me what books of his I had in stock, and would I please bring as many copies of each as possible to him at the hospital. Accordingly I went there on the morning of January 2nd. I found his daughter Katie in attendance, along with Harvey Brown, a young publisher who had issued a couple of pamphlets by Olson as well as some by Ed Sanders and other members of the group around Olson. There was also a minor New England poet and his wife who lived in Gloucester near Olson.

The following half hour after my arrival was extremely macabre and decidedly unpleasant as far as I was concerned. I had brought along several things for Olson to sign for me personally, mostly duplicating titles that I had sent him, with his permission, over a year earlier, which he had never gotten around to returning. Olson was a huge man—he was six feet seven inches tall—and was suffering not only from the imminent approach of death, but also from the indignity of the fact that his dentures could not be found. Apparently they had been lost or mislaid during his transfer from Boston to New York. He was becoming more and more frustrated at his inability to make us understand what he was saying, his anger mounting with each repetition. While I had corresponded with him, this was my first and only face-to-face encounter.

As soon as I walked into his room he mentioned the books I had sent him and said they were still under his bed in Gloucester. I told him not to worry about them, that they were trifles, and that he had more important things to think about. He then asked what titles I had brought, and I showed him the half-dozen or so different ones that I had in multiple copies. He immediately began to inscribe them in an extremely shaky hand, totally unlike his usual firm, sweeping script, one copy of each for the neighbor poet. I was very shocked when this one demanded a second copy of each, saying, "Do one for my wife too."

The man was very obviously on his deathbed, yet these greedy demands were being made, oblivious of the physical strain it was putting on him, let alone what else it might have caused. I was so appalled at this total lack of sensitivity that I immediately abandoned my idea of hauling out my group of books, and decided that I would ask for only one thing to be signed.

A silence then ensued, and I was in a quandary. How was I to broach the subject of payment? I had brought in nearly four hundred dollars worth of books, which I simply could not afford to give away. But then, how do you ask a dying man for payment? Finally I took the publisher aside and asked him what to do. He said to just tell Olson that I had to get back to the shop, and did he want to pay for the books now. I did this and left as soon as possible thereafter. Olson died one week later at the age of sixty.

Olson's funeral in Gloucester was a quasi-Roman Catholic service. It was attended by virtually all of the Beat group to whom he was more or less the paterfamilias. With these men in attendance, it was probably the most hirsute funeral on record in this century. The pallbearers were Allen Ginsberg, Joel Oppenheimer, Ed Sanders, Harvey Brown, and two others whose names I have forgotten. Everybody was dressed seriously. That is, within the norm for the group, meaning that Ed Sanders, for example, wore a turtleneck sweater, and Allen Ginsberg wore shoes—tennis shoes—perhaps as much for protection from the freezing rain as in homage to Olson. At that point in his career, Ginsberg was going barefoot most of the time.

Several of Olson's poems were read during the service, making it undoubtedly the only time the word "piss" was spoken aloud during a Catholic Mass. At the graveside, Allen started chanting "Elohim Adonai" from the Jewish burial service, ending with an agonized shriek that echoed off the low, gray, dull clouds. At the conclusion of the service, everyone repaired to Olson's favorite bar for a wake in order to end on an upbeat note.

Barely a month later Louise Bogan died suddenly. This was an enormous loss for me, for I had gotten to know her within weeks after taking over the Phoenix. She was one of the sources that Larry Wallrich had promised I would discover in time. Bogan had been for many years the poetry editor for the *New Yorker,* and in this capacity received as review copies virtually every new volume of poetry issued. Selling them was traditionally one of the perks of being a reviewer. Seldom did she want to keep any of them, and she periodically called me to come buy the lot, as she had done with Wallrich. She worked at a small desk in her bedroom, and the rather large stack of books, which always filled at least four standard shopping bags, were heaped up between it and the bedroom door. Once, when telephoning me about them, she said, in an off-hand manner, "You'd better come on up, I can't get the bedroom door shut." Then, thinking how that might sound, continued, "Oh dear, I hope no one is listening in. That sounds rather *louche.*"

She lived just a few blocks north of my residence in the Washington Heights area, so when the initial call from her came, I was very pleased that Larry had been correct about the fact that I would discover the sources, and especially one within walking distance of my apartment. I was also truly thrilled at the prospect of meeting her, as I had always held her poetry in high esteem, and had started collecting the few volumes she had published. A date was selected, but then she asked if I could come around early. When I asked how early, I was taken aback when she said, "Oh, say seven a.m.?"

As I've explained, in those days the shop stayed open until 11 p.m. and I had more than an hour's subway ride home, then had to eat a late supper and attend to personal matters before going to sleep around 4 a.m. I managed to get her to agree to 7:30 a.m., so it was a very sleepy book-buyer who rang her bell that first time. She lived on the sixth floor of an old, but well-maintained apartment building looking across the Hudson River to the Palisades of New Jersey. I knew what she looked like from photographs, but I was surprised how tall she was. As soon as she had shut the door she asked me if I would like a cup of coffee. Normally I never drank coffee, always preferring tea, but I accepted, hoping that it would keep me awake. Zowie, did it ever! It was the strongest I had ever tasted. I decided that this must be authentic down-East farm coffee (she was, of course, born and bred in Maine.)

After we had finished our coffee, I followed her into the bedroom-workroom and proceeded to go through the books piled around the desk. As I went through them, adding up prices, she would occasionally offer her opinion of the poet or the book. I was at first surprised that she couldn't stand Denise Levertov, who at that particular time was my favorite among current poets. I diplomatically kept my opinion to myself and continued sorting through the stack of books. Much later I realized that Bogen was a strict formalist, and as Levertov was one of the postwar school of poets using natural breath rhythms rather than the centuries-old standard metrics, I began to understand Bogan's dislike. This realization came to me after one of Bogen's very rare public appearances at the "Y" shortly before Christmas of 1968.

It was a miserable day—rain and sleet and wind—and as luck would have it, I was running a temperature and did not feel up to attending in such wretched weather. But Bogan had sent Marshall and me complimentary tickets as well as an invitation to the reception at Marie Bullock's afterward. It was a command performance which I could not refuse, especially as I was scheduled to go to her apartment the next morning for one of the periodic book-buying sessions. By the time the reading commenced I was feeling much better, and was able to enjoy it. She read superbly, prefacing each poem with a very short but cogent explanation of the origin or inspiration for it.

The food and drinks at Mrs. Bullock's (she was president of The Poetry Society of America) were excellent, and the "inner circle" of invitees was quite distinguished, including Glenway Wescott, Monroe Wheeler, Padraic Colum, Ralph Pomeroy, Robert Phelps, Jean Garrigue, and many others. Bogan was induced to read three more short poems, and concluded by emphasizing the value of form, saying, "Poetry is important, form is fun."

Then a discussion ensued about the various meters and forms available to a poet, Bogan stating that she felt the villanelle was almost impossible in English. At this a large red-headed woman interjected, "I wrote a beautiful villanelle recently."

Bogan just barely acknowledged hearing this interruption with a carefully modulated, "Yes, well," and went on with her remarks. The next morning during the book-buying I asked her who the red-headed woman was. "Oh, that was Isabella Stewart Gardner," was her reply. "Dreadful poet, but with a name like that you can get *anything* published in Boston.

Shortly after that I finished up my book-buying accounts, and asked her to inscribe one more book before I lugged the shopping bags to the nearest subway stop.

The routine was to be repeated three or four times each year until her death, but with a small, significant variation during the first year. On the second visit she offered coffee again, and surprised me by asking, "Would you like something in it?" I wasn't sure just what she meant, but decided that the polite thing to say would be, "Well, if you are. Whatever you are having will be fine."

Again I was surprised and just slightly shocked when she brought out a bottle and laced our mugs with some gin. I wasn't expecting alcohol, but I drank it with outward equanimity, and proceeded with our usual routine of adding up the totals, discussing one or two of the titles, and having her sign whatever books of hers I had been able to add to my collection since the last visit. The following visit at the end of the year was identical. but soon into the new year, she apparently felt that not only did she know me well enough by then, but she could also trust me, for this time no coffee was offered, but instead a glass of straight gin. I had never liked gin, preferring vodka, but as always I went with the flow.

It revealed something of her character in that, despite the fact that she had battled alcoholism during much of her emotional life, she was such a lady, a New England lady at that, that she waited well over a year before becoming familiar enough with me to let down her hair. Which once she did quite literally, opening her door for me before she wound her long hair into the usual bun at the back of her head.

She did not publish a great deal of work—actually issuing only six volumes of poetry in a career lasting over fifty-five years—and two of those were collected poems. She did a lot of reviewing, and published several volumes of criticism and translation. After I had started the Oblong Octavo series I asked her to join it, but she refused, only because she had no unpublished work to offer, explaining, "The aperture through which my poetry comes is so tiny."

Then, after a long silence, there was a small burst of *Three Songs* appearing in the *New Yorker*. These were exactly what I wanted, and invited her to come down to the Phoenix to discuss this over lunch with me and Marshall Clements, who was also a devotee of her work. This was in February, and she telephoned that morning to ask if we might postpone the meeting for a few days until it warmed up a bit, as it was a bitter, freezing day. Although disappointed, we of course acquiesced, only to be extremely saddened by her sudden death a few days later from a heart attack.

In March a memorial service was held at The American Academy of Arts and Letters, of which she had been a member. I recall how proudly she told of her election to the chair once occupied by Robert Frost. She felt that this was a validation of her work. I also recall how bitterly disappointed she was that her final volume, *The Blue Estuaries,* failed to win the Pulitzer Prize. She admitted that she really had expected to win, and had wanted to, but then terminated further discussion by commenting, "Well, just look at the type of poet who wins that prize," the disappointment and bitterness showing clearly in her voice. The Pulitzer that year went to Anthony Hecht for *The Hard Hours.*

About one hundred people attended the service, including Robert Lowell, W.H. Auden, Glenway Wescott, Robert Giroux, Robert Phelps, and May Swenson, as well as the readers, John Hall Wheelock (who had been instrumental in getting her first book, *Body of This Death,* published in 1923), William Maxwell, William Jay Smith, Richard Wilbur and Leonie Adams, with whom she was often paired and compared. Unfortunately Miss Adams' talk was embarrassing, as she rambled on, often disjointedly and incoherent, apparently in the belief that she was addressing a group of high school freshmen who needed to be told what poetry was. Fortunately the men were superb in their tributes, direct and simple. The affair closed with some Mozart piano works played by the poet Jean Garrigue's sister, Marjorie.

VII

Publications of the Phoenix

Publishing had never been part of my original plans or even hopes for the shop. But a proposal from my colleague James Carr provided us with an easy entry into the field with our joint publication of John Wieners' second book *Ace of Pentacles* in 1964. John was living in New York at the time, and regularly came into the shop with material to sell. He was virtually without income, and was always in need of cash. Once, during one of these transactions, I asked him why he had never published another book after the great success of his first, *The Hotel Wentley Poems,* a twenty-four-page pamphlet that had been published in California nearly a decade earlier.

"Nobody ever asked me," was his laconic reply. I remarked how sad that was, and continued with the purchase of what he had brought.

James Carr came in one evening some months later merely to visit, and at some point said that he was interested in the then emerging Beats, and would like to publish something by one of them.

"You know these guys," he said, "Why don't we go together on something. You get the manuscript and I'll do the publishing part."

This sounded interesting to me. I was sure we could get something from Wieners, and I agreed. But I had to wait until John's next appearance in the shop, for he had no telephone, and in fact I did not know exactly where he was living. He soon showed up however, and I relayed the proposal. John agreed immediately and a few days later he returned with a hefty accumulation of poems, enough to fill a substantial volume. After John left, I telephoned Carr, who came over the very next night and took the manuscript home to read. Thus we started the ball rolling. Since it was to be a joint publication, there arose a small problem as to the wording of the publishers. Carr did not have a shop per se, and operated from his apartment.

And it would look odd to have one personal name alongside "The Phoenix Book Shop." We finally decided simply to use both of our personal names. It thus came about that the first publication of the Phoenix Book Shop did not bear the shop's name.

We had planned to issue the book in three formats: paper, cloth, and a signed edition. There were one thousand paper, one hundred cloth, and seventy-five of the deluxe. This last figure corresponded to the number of pages of Wieners' manuscript, since we bound one page into each of the black leatherette deluxe copies. As it turned out, there were twelve over-runs, something not at all unusual in printing. So we decided to employ

John Wieners

these as an "Author's Edition" by having John write out a poem in holograph for each of these extra copies. The original "manuscript", as one customer complained, was actually his corrected final typescript. These extra dozen copies were never for sale but were retained for our personal use.

There is a lengthy coda to the history of this book. When I went to London in 1964 on my first such buying trip, I found that the Wieners book had made quite an impression on the literary avant-garde world in London as well as in the United States. Someone suggested that I visit Cape Goliard, a subsidiary of Jonathan Cape, one of the most prestigious publishers in England. I promptly did so and was very pleased that one of the officials of the firm, Tom Maschler, was quite receptive to the idea of there being a British edition under the Cape Goliard imprint. He asked for a six-month option, which I readily gave him. However, I never heard from him or the firm again, so two years later on my next trip to England, I met a young independent publisher whose Fulcrum Press had been issuing handsome editions of American poets, especially two by Gary Snyder. He told me that he was anxious to be able to include a Wieners book in his list. Since the option I had given Cape Goliard had long since lapsed, I now gave the rights to Fulcrum, who proceeded to set up type for it.

Then, after I got back, John came into the shop one evening with items to sell, something he did regularly. Among the items, to my horror, was a set of galleys of a *Selected Poems* by him including all of *Ace of Pentacles*. John, in all naiveté, had accepted a proposal from Mr. Maschler for such a book. Maschler apparently thought that the six-month option was still in force. At once I wrote to him that such was not the case, and explained to him that I no longer had control over the rights, nor did he, since they were now assigned to Fulcrum. This caused an impasse and Cape Goliard started pressuring me to withdraw the rights from Fulcrum. I was unwilling to do this, as Fulcrum was run by a young couple who had barely enough money to eat properly (as became obvious one day when they shared their lunch with me), let alone to suffer the financial loss such a withdrawal would entail.

And The Phoenix was also unwilling to authorize something that would effectively kill the sale of our remaining four hundred or so copies of our edition of the book. The original agreement for a British edition—as in all such transatlantic arrangements—was that it could not be offered for sale in the United States. But a *Selected Poems,* having no corresponding American counterpart, could be legally sold here. The resulting deadlock meant that John was being deprived of the possibility of income as well as publicity that could help his career. His peers, including Allen Ginsberg, starting asking me to withdraw my objection.

Eventually I arranged to meet Allen and explain the situation to him, as he had thought that I was simply being obstinate and refusing to coop-erate. When Allen learned that in fact I had no legal right to grant permis-sion to Cape Goliard, he stepped in and brokered an arrangement that resolved the impasse. Cape Goliard would purchase my remaining copies, effectively making *Ace of Pentacles* out of print, and they would also reimburse Fulcrum for whatever expenses they had incurred. This satisfied all concerned, and eventually John's *Selected Poems* made its appearance.

Late in 1965, Marianne Moore sent a young protégé, Jeff Kindley, to me, armed with a note praising his poems. After a couple of visits with him and a chance to read his poems, I decided that the Phoenix should publish them, especially as Miss Moore had promised to write an introduction for them. Thus the first book which actually bore the Phoenix imprint, *The Under-wood*, appeared in 1966, but not without a lot of heartache and tribulation.

First, Miss Moore changed her mind and decided not to write the promised introduction, but merely a dust jacket blurb. This was a severe disappointment as it reduced potential sales considerably. There existed a great many collectors of her work who would have bought copies with an introduction, but there were none whatever who collected books with dust jacket blurbs by her, since she had been overly generous with such.

Next, the printer used the wrong color on the dust jacket, and the artist, Lawrence Scott, was enraged that his design had been printed in green instead of red, as originally specified. Added to this, the binding machine had crumpled the first signature in all five hundred copies. So everything had to be redone. We also had twenty-six boxed signed copies as a deluxe edition. After all this, I am sorry to have to say that the book did not sell at all well, and when the shop closed twenty-three years later, most of the copies were still there. Disappointed by his failure as a poet, Kindley returned to the theater and authored the book for an Off-Broadway musical which, unfortunately, fared no better than the poems.

In 1966, on the next biennial visit to England I met Asa Beneviste, a British poet and small-press operator, who suggested that we collaborate on a book by Jack Hirschman, a rising young American poet. Having read his work and liking it, I agreed immediately on the co-publication of *Black Alephs* (which one of my customers thought was entitled *Black Olives*). Production was slow, and the book did not appear for almost another entire year. By that time production costs had mounted to a figure well beyond the original estimate; but Asa, without consulting me, had printed on the dust jackets the original retail price we had agreed upon, leaving me no room whatever to offer trade discounts to dealers. In all innocence he thought Hirschman's fame was so great that I would be able to sell all five hundred copies of the American imprint at full retail. He did reluctantly cut my share somewhat, but that merely made the venture break even after a dozen years.

While awaiting the completion of Hirschman's book, I kept casting about to find something unpublished by Gertrude Stein, my primary passion in modern literature. This was nearly impossible however, since Yale had seen to the publication of all her unpublished manuscripts in a series of nine hefty volumes. Somewhat earlier, before I became the proprietor of the Phoenix, I had received permission from Donald Gallup, her literary executor, to publish a small pamphlet of some letters by her, which I used as a personal Christmas greeting, but nothing further seemed available.

Then one lucky day I finally obtained for my collection copies of *The Psychological Review* in which her very first appearances in print had occurred in 1896 and 1898. these were her accounts of her experiments in automatic writing during her graduate studies in medicine at the Johns Hopkins Medical School in Baltimore. They had never been reprinted, and it occurred to me that these would be of interest to collectors and scholars alike, since very few if any academic institutions had files of obsolete medical journals from the previous century. Accordingly in 1969 I published them in a compact pamphlet entitled *Motor Automatism*.

In 1972 Gregory Corso showed me a quatrain he had just written about Christmas. I immediately saw its possibility as the shop's annual Christmas greeting, and offered to have it printed in an edition of four hundred copies—two hundred for each of us. So two hundred bore the shop's imprint, and two hundred bore Gregory's name as the sender. Always in need of cash, Gregory, when I handed him his copies, asked if I would buy one hundred of them back. Of course I was happy to do so, since all of mine would be sent out as Christmas keepsakes to my better customers, and I knew that sooner or later customers who were not on my preferred list would get wind of their existence and want copies.

Again in 1973 I tried publishing a small book of poems by Tim Reynolds, a poet whose work I admired and who had had two or three books published to good reviews, but nothing currently in print. This one proved to be the most difficult of all the titles the Phoenix issued, due to the fact that Tim went off to Europe and roamed about with no fixed

49

address. Communication was almost impossible, and numerous times my letters came back as undeliverable. On at least two occasions when I wired him desperately needed funds, he had been unable to remain at the address he had supplied, and the cabled money came back. The file on *The Women Poem* is thicker than that of all our other publications combined.

Three editions were done: paper, cloth, and twelve in a special binding—two for the Phoenix and ten for Reynolds, presumably one for each of the ten women celebrated in the poem. Again, it was not a commercial success with copies still on hand in 1988. This was to be the last of our ventures in trying to promote the careers of struggling young poets. By this time we were already embarking on two other publishing projects: the bibliographies, and what turned out to be a series, although not originally intended as such, the signed, limited poetry pamphlets which came to be known as "The Oblong Octavos."

The bibliographies, also not first thought of as a series, started with Marshall Clements' bibliography of the works of Michael McClure. Clements had become a fan of McClure's work, and in fact had developed a lengthy correspondence with him. Marshall was working at the Phoenix at that time, so it seemed natural for us to issue the booklet with the Phoenix's imprint. There was no clear-cut idea just then of it becoming the first in a series. there was an obvious need, if not for full-scale bibliographies, at least for comprehensive and reliable checklists of the younger writers who were already being assiduously collected. Thus Marshall's bibliography of the works of Michael McClure became the foundation stone of the series. From that time on until the closing of the shop, there was always a bibliography in progress, even though it took years to complete some of them.

While Marshall was completing the McClure, I started personally compiling a bibliography of the works of Gregory Corso. It was issued a year later in 1966 in a format identical with the McClure, in an edition of five hundred copies. It was barely off the press when George Butterick and Al Glover offered us their bibliography of Charles Olson. I happily accepted it and again planned five hundred copies. Unfortunately the binding machine chewed up one hundred of them, and sorry to say, the printer had already destroyed the plates, making another printing not economically feasible.

Then, only four weeks later, Anne Charters, a young woman unknown to me at the time, came to me with her completed bibliography of Jack Kerouac. Since I was personally not a fan of his work—the only one of the beats whose work did not thrill me—I was somewhat hesitant about publishing it. Luckily I did, for quite ironically it turned out to be the most successful of all our publications, in whatever genre, and the only one that made a profit. In fact, the five hundred copies sold out so quickly that we soon went into a second printing, and a few years later Annie (as she preferred to be called) updated it into a revised and expanded edition which this time we issued hardbound.

Then there was a gap of five years with no other offers being made, so I started work on the books of Denise Levertov, the touchstone poet for me. This took me quite a long time to complete due to the international nature of her career, which started in her native Britain during World War II. Considerable travel was involved in tracking down her early British works, as the British Library's copyright holdings were destroyed during the Blitz of London. Eventually, with trips to Brown University, Harvard, and the University of Nevada at Reno, it was finally completed with help from Miss Levertov herself, appearing in 1972.

Then came another offer, and we published David Streeter's work on the poet Ed Dorn. This was the only failure in the bibliography series. It seemed that after the initial enthusiasm which greeted his work, interest diminished quickly after his Gunslinger books came out, and when the shop closed in 1998 over half of the edition remained unsold.

Next I embarked on my major bibliographical effort, the bibliography of Gertrude Stein. No really adequate bibliography existed at that time. Virtually the only thing available was the 1941 Yale exhibition catalog compiled by Robert Haas and Donald Gallup, and it was long out of print. Dr. Gallup had announced that he was working on the Stein, and had even journeyed down from New Haven to go through my own holdings some time before I acquired the Phoenix. but other tasks preempted his time, notably the updating of his flawless bibliographies of Pound and Eliot, which I always used as models whenever I wasn't sure how to handle a bibliographic problem.

Some time elapsed, and I kept chafing at the bit, but also kept accumulating data as I uncovered it. Stein's centennial year was approaching in 1974, and I felt it would be the perfect time to publish a Stein bibliography. So, fearing it might cause a breach in my longtime friendship with

Donald Gallup, I took the bull by the horns and started serious work on it. I had completed at least a first draft of the "A" section early in 1974, and had to go to Yale to borrow certain key items for the Grolier Club exhibit which I was mounting for the centennial celebration. I took along this completed section to show him. Alas, he wasn't in his office that day, so I was forced to leave it on his desk.

To my intense relief, he promptly wrote back with his customary charm and graciousness, making some very helpful corrections and suggestions. Later I came to think that perhaps he might even have been relieved of the necessity for completing the Stein, busy as he was with many editorial duties involved with Yale's publication of works by Stein and O'Neill among others. This time we issued the book clothbound, it being too large to be practical as a paperback. I'm afraid my hopes were a bit sanguine, for I had two thousand copies printed. Actually I had planned on only one thousand, but when I learned that an additional thousand would cost only two hundred dollars more, I went for it. It did sell well, for when the shop closed fourteen years later, there were only a little over three hundred copies remaining. Recently the firm of Quill and Brush published my revised updating in a handsome, fully illustrated edition.

The last of our bibliographies was Katherine McNeill's study of the works of Gary Snyder, which appeared in 1983, after some three years of intensive work and correspondence. We had actually announced two others, one on Kenneth Patchen and one on John Ashbery. But it soon developed that my friend and colleague Paul Appel had also announced a Patchen bibliography. When I learned of this conflict, I withdrew in favor of Paul, in deference to our friendship which was more valuable to me than any profit which might have accrued from the Patchen work.

The other, the work on John Ashbery, proceeded well enough with the compiler, David Kermani, spending much time going through my own extensive Ashbery collection. But as publication time approached he began making demands that the Phoenix could not afford, such as wanting five thousand advertising fliers printed and mailed out, acid-free paper used, extensive ads taken in trade journals, and such like. Bibliographies rarely pay their own way, and while I did not mind not making a profit on them, I wasn't in a position to lose money. Accordingly, by mutual agreement, the contract was canceled and

Kermani found another publisher, Garland. Ironically, as far as I could learn, the only one of the demands that Garland actually granted was the use of acid-free paper.

Now we come to my favorite of all the various types of publishing that we did—the series which came to be known as The Oblong Octavos. It did not begin its life as a planned series. The history of the first two, Marianne Moore's *Tipoo's Tiger* and W.H. Auden's *Two Songs* will be recounted in the sections on these two poets. All of the pamphlets were horizontal in format, printed on fine papers, usually Fabriano, and most by William Ferguson of Boston.

They were bound in a variety of handmade papers produced abroad. Throughout the series there were always one hundred numbered and signed copies printed for sale, and twenty-six lettered and signed, reserved half for the Phoenix and half for the poet, none of the latter for sale. For practical purposes I always had one hundred and fifty printed, for quite often it would happen that copies were ruined in the binding, or even spoiled in the signing. These were generally not signed, but in a couple of instances when the poet was not going to be available when the pamphlets were completed, I would have the printer send the colophon sheets to the poet for signing before binding. These over-runs were carefully marked *hors commerce* so that they could never be confused with the regular edition.

After the overwhelming success of the Moore and the Auden, I began to think about continuing publishing similar pamphlets by some of my favorite poets. I was trying to think who among them might be amenable to the idea. At that time John Ashbery's reputation was beginning to take off. I had been very impressed with his first three books, but he had not as yet had a signed limited edition. What was more to the point was that I knew him fairly well, since he lived next door to me. So I asked John if he would like to join the group. He immediately replied in the affirmative and, since he was going out of town for an extended period, mailed me a sheaf of new poems. Unfortunately I did not like them as, quite frankly, I could not make head nor tail of what he was trying to convey. So I sent them back, asking if he had any others. He replied, "I knew you wouldn't like them. I just KNEW it!" But he also sent some others which I did like.

Thus, *Sunrise in Suburbia* appeared in 1969. The group of poems which I had turned down appeared not too much later in a somewhat similar series being issued by Diane di Prima. Hers were interestingly produced in holographic facsimile of the poet's manuscript. Our Ashbery title had appeared just after the beginning of the year, and was followed in quick succession by *Complaint* by Richard Wilbur, *Three Poems* by W.S. Merwin, and *The Poet Dreaming in the Scholar's House* by Howard Nemerov. Mr. Wilbur paid me the compliment of allowing me to choose a Latin epigraph or one in English. I opted for the English one on the basis of the fact that most Americans could not read Latin, and I myself, despite seven years of it in school, was still unable to handle the language.

An anecdote concerning the Wilbur should be mentioned. We had once approached Vladimir Nabokov about the possibility of doing one of his groups of verse, not really expecting success. We were not too surprised when we received a letter from his wife Vera, saying that he never signed anything except for close personal friends, and would never consider signing anything on a commercial basis. In a discussion one day with his cousin, the composer Nicholas Nabokov, the latter told me how indignant he was that Vladimir wouldn't even sign letters to him, despite their having grown up together on their grandparents' estates in pre-Revolutionary Russia, and had Vera sign all the correspondence.

Obviously Nabokov was almost paranoid about letting his signature out into the world. Nonetheless, Vladimir had actually read the Wilbur poem I had sent him as a sample, for a number of years later, in a volume of his essays and interviews called *Strong Opinions,* he was asked by the interviewer if he had read any books lately that had impressed him. His reply was the only thing he had read that had made any impression on him was a pamphlet published by the Phoenix Book Shop, a poem by Richard Wilbur entitled *Complaint.* High praise indeed!

The Merwin was the result of a pleasant surprise. W.S. Merwin came into the shop one evening and said he had learned that we were publishing signed limited editions and wondered if we would be interested in publishing something of his. Most assuredly.

I had admired his poetry and collected it myself, so would probably have gotten around to approaching him in any event. The following year we finally got to publish Robert Duncan, also an intimate friend. I had requested something from him much earlier, and he had readily assented. But for over a year nothing was forthcoming from California. I became somewhat miffed when Margie Cohn announced a Duncan title in her Crown Octavo series. I felt angry that Robert would send her something when he hadn't fulfilled his promise to me. I was considerably mollified when I learned that what he had sent Margie was a very long prose piece that would have been totally unsuitable for our use. Later on that year he did send a superb poem, *Achilles' Song,* and even offered to design the cover and to make individual drawings in each of the lettered copies.

The following year Gary Snyder, not to be outdone, also offered to design the cover of *The Blue Sky* as well as to draw a small figure of a running flute player to be used to indicate stanza breaks. In the chapter on Snyder I have related how this publication very nearly had to be abandoned, and there is no need to repeat it here.

While Gary's book was in progress, Michael McClure contributed his *Plane Pomes,* written as always in his usual format of lines being centered on the page. This would have caused each poem to be split into two pages, each with abnormally large, wide margins. I solved this dilemma simply by having the booklet bound at the top, opening similar to a steno pad. This allowed each poem to appear handsomely on a single page with normal margins. I had selected a Japanese rice paper looking vaguely like clouds for the cover, Michael was enchanted and wrote back that he had spread the entire edition, all one hundred and twenty-six copies, out on the floor when he received them for signing, saying that the result looked exactly like the cloud formation outside the plane window as he was actually composing the poems.

The following year John Wieners' *Youth* appeared. It was at this point that the series received its official name, The Oblong Octavo Series. I had never intended a name, but a Midwestern university wrote asking for a series name. It seemed that their accounting office had a rather odd requirement: their library was not allowed to subscribe to a series of publications unless the series had a name! So after a little thought I settled on the rather obvious, hoping my friend and colleague, Margie Cohn, would not be too unhappy about the perfectly obvious spin-off from her justly famous Crown Octavo Series. Apparently she was not, for she never mentioned the subject other than to subscribe for several copies.

In 1970 there were two more: Tim Reynolds giving me a portion of a work in progress, *Tlatelolco,* and just in time for Christmas, Louis Zukowsky's

John Ashbery and John Yau

Initial, a welcome departure from his obsession with the letter "A". It was in large part a tribute to the Met's chorus master David Stivender, whose friendship with Zukovsky had come about through my introducing them.

The following year there appeared only one title, Gregory Corso's *Ankh.* This caused a struggle with the Library of Congress' copyright office. Gregory wanted simply the actual ankh symbol for the title. The copyright office rejected the application, saying a picture could not be registered as a title. It took three letters to convince them that the ankh symbol was not an illustration, but a character in a recognized, albeit defunct, alphabet.

In 1973 I asked Allen Ginsberg for something. He agreed but with the stipulation that he would do it only if I would publish something by his lover, Peter Orlovsky, who, while having been printed in magazines, had no book to his credit. I agreed at once. To have a signed Ginsberg in the series was certainly a coup, but to have as well Peter Orlovsky's first book was an additional bit of good luck.

Later in 1973 Two long-desired projects came to fruition. I had for several years been pursuing two of my top favorite poets to get them to join the series. While both of them had tentatively agreed, both were out of the country either all or most of the time, and communication was slow and difficult at best. Both had contracts with their respective publishers who were very reluctant to allow anyone else to issue publications by these poets.

And, finally, both were under contract to the *New Yorker* magazine for first refusal on all new work.

I am referring to James Merrill and Elisabeth Bishop. While I did not mind if the poems had been printed in a magazine, I did insist that whatever was issued in the series would be its first book appearance. so, in the case of these two, it meant that there was ordinarily not much time between magazine appearance and appearance in the poets' next volumes. There was very little "window of opportunity" as modern parlance terms it. to get the permission of both publishers in a relatively short apace of time was not easy. And we had to do all of these when each poet was reachable by mail.

Fortunately for me, Miss Bishop had finally returned permanently to the United States after may years of living abroad in a remote area of Brazil. She was now living in Boston and had become quite familiar with my printer, Bill Ferguson. This neatly solved one major problem, for she was adamant about overseeing every step of the production. When the printing was completed and the time came for Bishop to sign the copies, I flew up to Boston. Ferguson assured me that he would be happy to take care of it for me and my presence was not necessary. but I insisted, since I realized that this would be a unique opportunity for me to get all of my personal collection of her books signed as well.

With Merrill, I had only to walk two blocks from my residence to accomplish this, although it was to sign the colophon sheets only, as he was leaving for his annual stay in Greece the next day. All of my own personal collection had already been inscribed, so on this occasion I took along the shop's guest book to which he graciously added. The Bishop book, entitled simply *Poem* appeared first. It has since become her most often reprinted poem, and the booklet is the only signed edition in her entire *oeuvre.* Merrill's book was entitled *Yannina* and it too has often been reprinted. In the two decades that have elapsed since the issuance of these two titles, they have become the most sought-after (and most highly priced) in the entire series.

By this time I had issued something by nearly all of the authors I wanted in the series with the exception of Diane di Prima. It was two years before we finally worked out something with Diane, in the form of *Loba As Eve,* a portion of her long, ongoing 1975 poem about the legendary Loba. Although beautifully produced, it was, unfortunately, somewhat of a financial calamity, since she wanted a cover design by her friend Josie Grant, who also had to be paid. This was in addition to the extra expense of the die-cut for the cover illustration.

Only two titles remained. In 1976 Galway Kinnell contributed *Three Poems* to the series, and then, after a lapse of another three years, I rounded out the series with the twentieth volume, Amiri Baraka's *Amtrak.* Amiri had been a friend from the earliest days, when he was known as LeRoi Jones. We had drifted apart during his more militant days as a Black activist, but later on we got back to something which resembled the old friendship. This made a nice cut-off point, so 1979 saw the close of the series.

There were a few regrets that I could not include anything by Adrienne Rich. Over the years I wrote to her three times but never received an answer. I was also disappointed that my old friend Denise Levertov would join only on the condition that I turn over the entire proceeds to one of her charities, something that we simply were not strong enough financially to afford. I've already chronicled Nabokov's refusal. Finally, Christopher Isherwood also declined. Of course he wasn't a poet and I doubt that most people even know that he had published a small number of poems. In fact, his first appearance in print was a poem published in a series known as Public School Verse, in 1923, with a poem entitled *Mapperley Plains.* Other precocious prep school boys in this same anthology were A.L. Rowse and H. Graham Greene. Two years later Auden also made his debut in the series, although his pleasure must have been somewhat dimmed by the editor's misspelling of his name as "W.H. Arden." I knew that Isherwood had received one of the Auden pamphlets and I wrote to him suggesting that it might be fun to gather all his poems and have the small pamphlet entitled *The Complete Poems of Christopher Isherwood.* While he enjoyed the humor inherent in that title, he wrote back that he would be too embarrassed in that his poems weren't of a sufficiently high caliber to join the group. He did, however, write out one in holograph for me in the shop's guest book.

There now remains the last series, the Christmas pamphlets. As with all the others, I had no intention of making a series out of them. When I acquired Auden's library my cousin, William S. Wilson, suggested that for the sake of posterity I should catalog it. Unfortunately this was simply far too impractical, given the great volume of it, and the necessity to move most of it as quickly as possible, if only to get the space to walk in. So I

Gregory Corso

made notes as to the general outlines of his library. Then one of my customers, the late Herman Abromson, suggested that I issue it as a Christmas keepsake, the collecting of which was one of the many fields of interest to him in his wide-ranging collecting activity.

I took his suggestion and in 1975 issued *Auden's Library* in a print run of three hundred copies, nearly all of which were mailed out to my customers. I have now greatly expanded this memoir as one of the chapters in this book. It was so well received that the following year I offered some of my memories of Marianne Moore in *Marianne Serves Lunch,* which has also formed the basis of a chapter herein. This rather naturally turned the Christmas tokens into an annual series of ten, from 1975 until 1985, with the exception of 1984. While I did include memories of Alice B. Toklas, Olga Rudge, and Michael McClure, not all were about literary personalities. One—*Rider Haggard's She*—is also printed *in toto* in this volume, as is another, *Faulkner on Fire Island. Six Favorites,* the 1982 volume, describes six of my most cherished books and tells why they are among my favorites. And one has nothing whatever to do with literature but relates the adventures of my friend Kenneth Doubrava and myself in gathering wild mushrooms in such widely varied locales as a tiny hamlet in the Tyrol portion of the Austrian Alps and West Twenty-sixth Street in New York City. And one came about because the pressure of time prevented me from writing anything in time to get it printed. So I simply gathered together several of my photographs I had made of some of my author friends and issued it under the title *Ten Tintypes and a Tiger*. In the past few years I have been both flattered and amused to see these pamphlets appearing in rare book dealers' catalogs at increasing prices.

There was one publication which was totally different from anything else that we issued. This was *Greenwich Village As It Is* by Djuna Barnes, an article from her days as a freelance journalist. It had appeared in the October 1916 issue of *Pearson's Magazine*. It had apparently been forgotten by Barnes, and in fact, was unknown to her bibliographer. When a copy came into the shop, I was struck by its importance and immediately wrote to Miss Barnes suggesting that it could be copyrighted, (the original work having long since entered the public domain,) and offering to publish it. I had no reply to any of my three letters, so I decided to publish it anyhow, complete with the series of woodcuts which had accompanied the article. It was done as one of the very first works printed by the then new Nadja Press, in an edition of three hundred copies. I sent Miss Barnes ten copies, along with the standard royalties on the entire edition, amounting to six hundred dollars, a respectable sum in those pre-inflation days. I never heard from her other than to get back the cashed check. I did hear that she told an acquaintance of mine who was doing some appraisal work her that she remarked, "Wilson should have known better." Whatever her opinion, it was one of our bestselling titles.

VIII

Farewell to the Phoenix

I never had any intention of retiring, nor did I ever dream that I would have to close the Phoenix. Life in New York had been getting steadily worse and worse. Crime kept increasing, and the city was falling apart. I had been burglarized four times at three different residences. I was mugged coming up out of the subway. The shop had been burglarized at both locations, and I was twice held up at gunpoint in the shop.

In addition to all this, the city itself began to make it impossible to comply with new laws. In a misguided attempt to keep the city clean (since the sanitation workers for quite some time had failed to do so) a law was passed requiring all property owners to keep the gutter in front of their property clean. No matter how hard you tried, this was an impossibility unless you maintained watch around the clock. For example, I would sweep and clean the gutter in front of my house every morning, and then go to work. When I came home at night there would be a fine notice affixed to my door because someone had thrown a cigarette package in the gutter at some point during the day. I was left with the choice of either paying the fine or fighting it down at city hall. This would take up most of the day, and was more costly than paying the fine. But you got a fine almost every week. Obviously, this law had not been clearly thought out before being enacted. There were other harassments that I won't go into.

I decided in the early 80s to think about leaving the city , and started looking for a home on the Eastern Shore of Maryland, my ancestral turf. It was three years before the right one came along. At first we used it for weekends in the summer, and in the winter we came down once a month to check on everything. Despite our hopes for a turnaround in the city it didn't happen, so we started to move entirely out of New York. We put our town house up for sale, and I began to cast about for someone to buy the Phoenix. I wanted someone who would continue it more or less along the lines for which it had become world famous: a place receptive to the avant-garde in literature and where you could also find the great works of the past

At first I offered it to Matthew Monaghan, who at the time was working at the Gotham Book Mart. Matthew was knowledgeable in the field, and was also personable. He was also anxious to venture out on his own at some point. He considered the proposition for some time, but he and his wife finally decided that buying their own home had priority over acquiring a shop. Unfortunately, it was not long after this that Matthew died prematurely of encephalitis.

Next I tried offering it to a part-time book dealer, Brad Morrow, who had come from California and started a very fine and much respected literary quarterly. He took six months to decide that he really didn't like the idea of being tied to a shop on a full-time basis. His refusal was charmingly couched in a letter that ended, "Anyway, you're too hard an act to follow," perhaps the nicest compliment I've ever received. Not long after this, one of my customers who was also a part-time dealer told me he knew of a young woman school teacher who wanted to be out of the school system for obvious reasons, and might be interested in taking over the shop. When we met, I liked her immensely but wondered about the practicality of it. While she was very well-read in modern literature, she did not have any actual experience in running a business, and also had only a smattering of knowledge of first editions. However we both decided that she should sit in for a few hours every day and see how things went. She turned out to be a quick learner, and it wasn't long before we both felt that the transfer of the Phoenix to her would work out very well.

We then started legal negotiations. This took quite some time, but finally we reached an agreement on all the terms. Then came the tricky part—persuading the landlord to accept her as a tenant when the lease expired nearly two years hence. First of all, he had advised me that the increase in rent at that time would be a staggering one. I tried negotiating that point, but to no avail. However my would-be successor decided that she would accept the new figure if the landlord would give her a two-year lease instead of the proposed five years as had been previously worked out for three successive leases. We had then to persuade him to cancel my current lease and issue her a new one. This he agreed to at once, since he would be getting his rent increase a year earlier.

So all the preparations were made, and a date set for the transfer of the lease. Then to our total shock he telephoned up one day before the date to say that he had changed his mind and would not accept her as a tenant. This despite the fact that she and her husband had given him copies of their tax return proving that they had a very substantial income, and could clearly afford the lease. He gave no reason. We were both stunned. However the landlord was adamant, and our agreement dissolved over night. She had spent an entire year learning the ropes, and had quit her teaching job.

I was then left with the problem of what to do next. I had already sold my New York house, and being unable to find a suitable room to rent, had moved into the shop, where I slept on a piece of foam rubber in the back. There was only a toilet and washbowl, with no tub or shower facilities, and only a two-burner hot plate for meals. Two poet friends came to my rescue temporarily. Allen Ginsberg was going off on tour and let me use his apartment for weeks. Following this, Eve Merriam lent me hers for two months. Obviously, push had come to shove. I was forced to face the unbearable thought that I would have to be the one to kill the Phoenix, a shop that had been in existence nearly six decades under five different owners.

I set about trying to sell the inventory, which was massive by then. I hurriedly issued two more catalogs, and also advertised a half-price sale on everything in the shop. This sold off a lot of material, but there still remained an enormous number of books. I got in touch with Larry McMurtry who, in addition to writing great novels, had two book shops of his own, one in Washington, D.C., and one in his native Texas. I had met him a couple of times, and knew that he liked buying large quantities of books for his shops. We agreed on a price, but then a monkey wrench was thrown into the works. Hollywood went on strike, and the filming of *Lonesome Dove* was put on hold indefinitely. He had planned to use the money from this to pay for the Phoenix stock. We waited for some time, but the Hollywood strike showed no signs of a settlement so Larry told me that if I could not wait indefinitely, to sell it to someone else.

This finally happened when another Washington dealer who had more than one shop agreed to my price, on the condition that he could pay for it in twelve monthly installments. Having pretty much exhausted my options, I agreed to this, and he sent an enormous truck to pack up the Phoenix. Overnight the shop was empty. I then spent a couple more weeks selling off the equipment and shelving, and at last, endured the unendurable—I turned the key in the lock of the Phoenix Book Shop for the last time. It was on a fine autumn day in mid-October, 1988 that I walked away and never looked back.

Only three small remarks remain to tie up all the loose ends. The lady who had wanted to buy the shop did buy my extensive bibliographic reference library and went into the mail-order business from her apartment. Larry McMurtry eventually got the Phoenix inventory anyhow, buying it from his D.C competitor after the Hollywood strike was over. And the intractable landlord got what was coming to him—the shop remained unrented for two and a half years after I left. And even then he had to divide it into two smaller shops. The right half became a video rental store, with racks of cassettes where once had been poetry. In the other half, where formerly had been shelves of first editions of some of the twentieth century's greatest literary masterpieces, and where my desk had been located, around which had congregated many Pulitzer and Nobel prize winners, there was now the ultimate ignominy of a dry-cleaning establishment, with the neighborhood's clothing traveling back and forth on a mechanical rack.

IX

L'Envoi

Now that I have come to the end of my memories of what it was like to run the Phoenix for nearly three decades, I am afraid that I have been totally unable to capture or portray the fun and joy of that time, despite hardships, disappointments, and lost opportunities. I count myself more than lucky. I was truly blessed, more so than I could ever have dreamed possible, to live and work among poets, many of who are truly great, truly immortal. I had always, from my teenage years onward, longed to be a great, important writer. I can remember working in the university library at Johns Hopkins in order to pay part of my tuition, standing in the stacks, day-dreaming a la Walter Mitty, staring at the shelves, imagining books written by me, trying to see where I would fit alphabetically—somewhere between Thornton wilder and William Wordsworth!

But the Muses, in their capricious wisdom, did not grant me the gift. After floundering in several extremely diverse careers, I was fortunate enough to find my true métier in the world of books and literature, and at a time that was exciting and has turned out to be an important era in the history of American literature. To me it wasn't work. I was able at last to make a living at something that I loved doing. Long hours meant nothing. Sometimes I worked twelve hours a day, or even longer. I had to force myself to lock the door.

I remember arguing with my accountant for years about his insistence that I establish an I.R.A. account for my retirement. I kept telling his that I was never going to retire, and I truly believed that. After all, the great booksellers who were my role models—Frances Steloff, Margie Cohn, Mabel Zahn—had all worked right up to the day they died. I intended to do the same. But Fate, in the form of a greedy landlord, decreed otherwise, forcing me to close the book shop, which had been in existence since 1931, in the fall of 1988.

In the first chapter of this book I paid tribute to Frances Steloff for her extraordinary kindness on the first day of my tenure. It was part of a friendship that endured over the years. In 1986, three years before her death at the age of 101, a superb documentary film was made about her long career running the Gotham Book Mart. I was privileged to be invited to the premier screening. Unfortunately Frances was not well enough to attend, so afterwards I wrote the following letter to her:

Dear Frances:

Last night I saw the film about you, and , of course, was charmed by it, and in some places, moved to tears. I was sorry that you were not able to be there to accept congratulations. So I am writing this letter to you.

Without bragging, I think that more than anyone else in the audience, I could identify with what you were saying. I have always considered myself one of your children. It took me a long time to find my way to my proper calling. Although trained in English literature, for many years I denied my true self, and spent valuable time wasting it in other endeavors. But eventually my true calling made itself so insistent that I forsook the so-called glamorous world for the world of books and writers—and have never been happier.

When I first bought the Phoenix, it was not a literary shop but I worked assiduously to convert it to such as quickly as possible. I had two touchstones for guidance. If I faced a decision regarding a business practice I tried to think what my father (a successful hardware merchant) would have done. But when it came to decisions on what books to buy, I always asked myself, "What would Frances do?"

And the answer always came loud and clear. It was to have faith in the new generation, the ones scorned by the academics and the establishment. And it most certainly paid off. At the time I was getting started, it was the Beatniks and the Black Mountain poets who were doing the interesting work. Following this adherence to the ultra moderns paid off, just as it did with your adherence to Pound., Stein, Joyce, Eliot, Miller, etc. And when I say "paid off" I am not speaking of money, I mean in the friendships that developed with the writers, especially poets, whose work I championed by buying it, cataloguing it, advising universities to buy it, and so forth. I now count among my dearest friends many world-esteemed authors who had to struggle for recognition then.

Now, as soon as you are back in the shop, I want to come up and give you a big hug and kiss and tell you in person why I give thanks for the first day I walked into the Gotham Book Mart.

Frances replied:

Dear Bob,

Thank you so much for your very thoughtful and charming letter. I too have very fond memories of your many visits to GBM so many years ago. It is nice to know that the book treasures you acquired from us have found a home in which good books are truly loved.

It is of course difficult to capture in just thirty minutes of film all that has happened to me and GBM in ninety-five years. I am glad to know that you found it so meaningful. That pleases me.

Reading your letter convinced me that you must certainly be considered one of the "wise men" for you seem to have benefitted more than most. It makes the many years of hard work seem the more worth while when I receive letters such as yours.

Do come for a visit in three or four weeks. It will be nice to see you again.

Sincerely,
Frances

Seeing Shelley Plain

For the benefit of readers who have never visited the Gotham Book Mart I should explain that her phrase "wise men" refers to the sign outside the Gotham Book Mart which bears the legend "Wise men fish here," making me treasure her letter all the more.

There is a stanza in Robert Browning's poem *Memorabilia* which has stuck in my memory ever since my undergraduate days at Johns Hopkins University more than fifty years ago:

> "Ah, did you once see Shelley plain,
> And did he stop and speak to you
> And did you speak to him again?
> How strange it seems, and new!"

Well, it was worth all the hard work, hold-ups, burglaries, floods, disappointments, all the petty disasters of life, to be able to answer with a resounding "Yes—yes—YES!

"Of course I did see him plain, And not only Shelley, but the whole damn crew!"

Part Two

W. H. Auden

"Thank you for your letter. Please call me at GR3-0331. Best time between 9 and 9:30 a.m. W. H. Auden." With this terse, succinct response to my request in 1964 to have some books autographed began an acquaintance which terminated only with his death many years later. In between I was to see him two or three times a year, generally at his apartment on St. Mark's Place on New York's Lower East Side, occasionally at readings, or rarely at the book shop. I myself had lived for a few years just around the corner, on East Sixth Street, Unfortunately for me, at that time I was still suffering from all the intensive reading I had been required to do to obtain my bachelor's degree in three years instead of the customary four—a necessity caused by the lowering of the draft age to eighteen shortly after our entry into World War II. As a result, in the ensuing years I read little aside from the *New Yorker* or the occasional book by S.J. Perelman or Max Schulman. Certainly nothing more serious, and definitely no poetry. I had been an English and American Lit. major, and had pretty well read the entire corpus of literature in English from *Beowulf* down to such then current authors as Steinbeck and Saroyan, and even Spender and Auden. By the time I had gotten to more serious reading, I had moved to the other side of town.

On this initial visit I mentioned how much the neighborhood had changed in the few years since I had lived there. While it could hardly be termed "gentrification," (the word had not yet been invented,) the old ethnic food stores -Polish, Ukrainian and Jewish—were giving way to coffee houses, boutiques, and discos. The term "East Village" was now the accepted name for the area centered around St. Mark's Place, which in itself is a misnomer, for it is not a "place" in the usual sense of the word, but is actually nothing more grand than the name customarily given to the part of Eighth Street that lies east of Fourth Avenue.

The apartment was in an ancient brownstone on the north side of the street. the ground floor had once housed the press of the Communist newspaper *Novy Mir,* closely affiliated with Leon Trotsky at one time. Auden seemed to believe that this fact gave the building an historic cachet, for he mentioned it frequently. His own apartment was two flights up—the usual sort one outside and than a very long steep one inside until you reached his landing, with the ubiquitous sheet-iron door painted a deep brownish red. You entered into what had once been a foyer, but now had no discernible function other than housing a table and two chairs, all heaped with overflowing burdens of books and papers. He usually ate his meals at this table.

To the right was the front room facing south out onto the street. It had two tall windows (the ceilings were nearly fourteen feet high.) These windows appeared never to have been cleaned since Auden moved into the place, for even on the brightest, sunniest day the light that filtered through the grime was brown and dim at best. This room had a desk in it but it, like the foyer table, was so heaped with books, newspapers, magazines and accumulated correspondence in such profusion that no one could possibly have worked at it. On the far wall were floor-to-ceiling bookshelves crammed to overflowing.

To the left of the entrance was his principal room, his living room, the largest room in the apartment. On its left wall was a long, decrepit sofa, with a brick replacing one broken-off missing leg, and with the stuffing coming out of several holes in the upholstery. One of the seat cushions had a large hole burned in it, probably by a carelessly dropped cigarette, which was now surrounded by a water stain, probably from a martini hastily used to extinguish the blaze. The two ends of the sofa had large plywood panels, extending all the way up to the ceiling, creating a sort of box-like feeling. On the internal sides of these sheets of plywood were large framed pencil sketches of Elizabeth Mayer, his one-time hostess on his arrival in America, as well as his translator-collaborator on many occasions but most notably on the monumental translation of Goethe's *Italian Journey.* He apparently was

W. H. Auden's apartment

rather proud of this part of his work, for he showed me his copy on more than one occasion. Alas for me, I was never able to locate a copy until after his death, although he did give me a proof copy of the paperback edition, which he gladly signed. Remembering my own days in a similarly anti-quated building on my own first arrival in New York, I realized that the plywood sofa panels provided protection against the strong, cold drafts of air that were inevitable in these ancient buildings during the winter.

On the opposite wall was a fireplace, no longer in working condi-tion, surrounded also by floor-to-ceiling bookshelves, which, like their coun-terparts in the front room, were jammed to overflowing. In one corner was a very old phonograph flanked by two occasional chairs and a couple of small tables, all heaped with phonograph records, mostly seventy-eights. An ordinary cocktail table in front of the sofa completed the furnishings in this room. On the fireplace mantel sat a vase with three peacock feathers in it and a ceramic bull rather in the style of Picasso's pottery. At either end of the sofa were doors leading into the bathroom and kitchen. Further to the left of the kitchen entry was a small alcove, holding even more bookshelves and a large quantity of empty picture frames. Next to it was a small bedroom through whose open door one could easily see a rumpled, unmade bed , the sheets of which were decidedly gray. To put it in the kindliest light possible, Auden had priorities that were greater than housekeeping.

In the midst of this near-squalor was one magnificent art treasure— an original etching hand-colored by William Blake, depicting Jehovah descending from the clouds of heaven with a pair of calipers in hand, one of Blake's most famous works. This was one of the few possessions that Auden obviously treasured, for he pointed it out to me on almost every visit I made. At our penultimate meeting, when Auden was preparing to return to England, I noticed at once that it was no longer on the wall. I asked if he had sold it along with some other art works which he was parting with. He replied that no, indeed, Chester had hand-carried it onto the plane to their house in Kirschstettin, In Austria. Unfortunately, after Chester Kallman's death it disappeared, and neither Auden's or Chester's executors has been able to trace its whereabouts.

There is one other item that Auden treasured that has also disappeared, the complete original manuscript score by Igor Stravinsky for the opera *The Rake's Progress,* for which he and Chester had written the libretto. Stravinsky, in an uncharacteristic burst of generosity, had given it to Auden as a mark of his esteem. Auden showed it to me a couple of times, once asking, "You know about these things; what do you think it's worth? It's my insurance against some astronomical medical bill."

I told him that I had just recently seen one bar of music in Stravinsky's hand being offered for one thousand dollars in an autograph dealer's catalog, so he could compute the value by counting the number of bars in the manuscript. He seemed satisfied that it would bring an enormous price if he had to part with it.

This exchange led to the subject of opera and to my astonishment, he launched into a violent, vitriolic denunciation of Rudolf Bing, at that time the general manager of the Metropolitan Opera. Apparently his experience with Bing during the American premiere of *The Rake's Progress* had been extremely unpleasant. As much as he loved opera, he vowed that he would never cross the threshold of the Met while Bing was still the incumbent. I protested that he was missing some truly great performances, mentioning Birgit Nilsson's incomparable Isolde. He chuckled and said that he couldn't possible see her as Isolde because "She looks so horribly middle-class that she can't be Isolde *OR* Brunnhilde."

Visits to Auden were all scheduled at tea-time, since he habitually rose early and worked until lunch time. Knowing of his English birth and upbringing, I rather naturally expected to be served tea. But it never happened. "Tea" was either very strong coffee, or more usually, martinis even stronger. These were his favorite drink, and he once confessed to me that he kept not only the glasses, but also the gin and vermouth in the refrigerator so that there would be no need to dilute the drinks with ice. Not being an experienced martini drinker myself, I could barely navigate my way back to the shop after three of them at that initial visit.

The experience of having recently published the pamphlet of Marianne Moore's *Tipoo's Tiger* had been so exhilarating that I had just begun to think about issuing another one, and had started wondering just who might be impressed enough by the fact that Moore had allowed me to publish one of her poems. It soon dawned on me that Auden was the next logical candidate. I knew him personally, and I also was aware that he had seen the Moore pamphlet, for during the signing of them Moore had inscribed one to Auden, and had asked me to mail it to him for her. Incidentally, it was *not* one of the things he disposed of when packing up for his return to England. So early in March of 1968 I asked him if he would be willing to participate. He agreed readily, adding, "Mind you, I'm not doing it for the money," and then added with a devilish grin, "I'm taking the money, of course, but I'm doing it out of friendship."

I was both delighted and flattered by this, and was very pleased when he handed me the typescript of two recent, totally unpublished poems entitled collectively *Two Songs*. It seemed very odd and almost unbelievable to me that, despite the fact that he was arguably the most distinguished living poet writing in the English language, his regular publisher, Random House, had never issued a signed limited edition of any of his many titles. In fact, he had been asked only twice to do so, and in both cases the size of the editions from the two small presses were extremely limited. thus, exactly as had been the case with the Marianne Moore pamphlet, it sold out almost at once as soon as it became known in the book trade. The day I took them to him to sign was marvelous for me. He was in great high spirits, being at his charming best, witty, discursive, and hospitable. This was in great contrast to his usual manner on the telephone, which was almost always abrupt bordering on rudeness. This I understood totally, for like myself he had a distinct aversion to the telephone, and did not like to use it as a means of communication beyond actual necessity.

Among the many topics that came up that afternoon, we somehow got to Robert Graves' recently published translation of *The Rubaiyat of Omar Khayyam.* Obviously Auden did not think very highly of it, saying, "The man is vain, madly vain."

The conversation than drifted to the visual arts, and once again he pointed out his treasured Blake etching. I then told him how I had happened to acquire a pornographic Cocteau drawing that had been laid into the deluxe, limited edition of Jean Genet's homosexual novel concerning a French sailor's secret love for his commanding officer, published as *Querelle de Brest.* I had located it at the request of a Pulitzer Prize-winning playwright. When I finally found one, no easy task since there had been only twenty-six examples, published more than twenty years earlier, the playwright refused to purchase it when I showed it to him, complaining that he could not have it framed to hang in his dining room. Auden was astonished, saying, "How extraordinary! He *must* have known what it should look like. Certainly he wasn't expecting a portrait of the Virgin Mary!"

It was not long after this that he made the dramatic decision to leave America and return to England. He rang me up one day and asked if in a general way I would be interested in purchasing the portion of his library which he did not wish to take with him to the "grace and favor" cottage that Oxford was going to provide for him as a sort of "poet in residence." Of course I immediately said, "Yes, indeed." He went on to say "There aren't any first editions. I'm not a book collector, you know, and I'm afraid I have the world's worst collection of awful poetry. I get things sent to me from all sorts of people unknown to me." He continued, saying that when he got things sorted out he would call me again.

Eventually the call came, a mutually convenient time was agreed upon, and over I went accompanied by Marshall Clements, who was then my assistant in the shop. We felt sure that however correct he might be about the awful poetry, he would have to be wrong about there being no first editions in his library. In the nature of things there would simply have to be some. At any rate, we would soon know.

When we got there, the apartment was in worse shambles than I had ever seen it. As Auden's friends and visitors can testify, that is saying something. He was probably the most untidy housekeeper in British literary history, not even excepting Dr. Johnson. A lot of his possessions had already been shipped to England or to his summer residence in Kirschstettin in Austria, and other things were being packed on the spot as we arrived. The ensuing chaos was, at the very least, formidable. To separate the books he wanted to keep from those he would discard, he had gone to the shelves and had thrown on the floor, quite literally, those he had decided he wanted to keep, with the discards remaining on the shelves for us. He was still at it when we walked in that first day. I shuddered inwardly a good many times when I saw some of the books that would be treasure to any bibliophile being tossed about carelessly and even kicked aside when a pile became too unwieldy. After a few more tosses, he announced, "Everything left on the shelves is for you."

I looked around the apartment. there were thousands of books left in every room—in the main living room, in the small foyer-dining area, in the front work room, and even in the small alcove near the kitchen. I made a hasty calculation and told him it would take me about a week, at least, to go through the lot and give him an estimate of how much I could pay. He looked both amused and surprised at the mere idea of such a procedure and said, "My dear chap, I don't want an estimate—just get the lot out of here so that I can start using the shelves for other things I have to sort out."

I was to pay him later when I had had time to go through the lot back at the shop. So then began four solid days of bundling and packing and moving them to the shop. I owned no vehicle at that time, making it necessary for me to borrow my cousin's station wagon. It took four trips, each time with the wagon loaded literally to the roof.

During all the time that this was going on, there was a constant stream of friends, students, reporters, and all manner of visitors coming to say farewell. Generally the information which he gave to each was pretty much identical, and I gradually began to notice two recurring themes: one was his reason for leaving America. He was afraid of having a coronary and lying on the floor for days before anyone discovered him. As we now know, his doctor had warned him that his heart was in bad condition, but of course most of his circle were not then aware of this fact. He was spookily prophetic about this, for that is just what happened in Austria, although the coronary occurred in a Viennese hotel to which he had gone for the night after a reading, not wanting to drive back home late at night.

The other point that he somehow managed to work into the conversation was on a much more humorous level. He repeated an anecdote told him by Dorothy Day, the intrepid editor of the *Catholic Worker* after her release from a stay in the New York Women's Prison on a contempt of court charge. Auden had so sympathized with her stand that he appeared on a television quiz show to earn enough money to pay her fine and obtain her release. Apparently the inmates were allowed showers only once a week, and on one such day Dorothy heard a prostitute on her way to the communal bath quote Auden's line "Thousands have lived without love, but not one without water." He was immensely pleased by this, and regarded it as his greatest success—to be quoted in prison by a convicted whore.

Occasionally during our bundling of the books, we would come across an important item that we felt sure he had mistakenly overlooked, and would miss eventually when he unpacked things in England, and would want to have sent to him. Such things as his own copy of *Collected Shorter Poems* in the unique leather binding cone for him by his publisher, Random House, complete with his manuscript revisions. so I went over to him, excused myself for interrupting his lunch of two fried eggs and a can of beer, and asked if he meant to leave it. He glanced at it quickly, and said that we were to take it, he did not need it.

Somewhat later another item showed up. Once again we felt that we had better ask, and this time Marshall was told, "My dear young man, when I said take everything, I meant EVERYTHING," emphasizing the point by punctuating the air with two small circles which he formed by closing his thumbs against his forefingers. After that, no matter what we discovered, we packed it up, rather gleefully in some instances, as for example a two-column loose-leaf compilation of some three hundred pages of his own favorite poems by other poets throughout the ages, all industriously and laboriously copied out in his own hand.

Once back at the shop there began a two-week examination of what his library contained. Of course it is impossible to make a totally accurate summary of what Auden's total library consisted of based on the two-thirds—his rejects—which came into our possession. Presumably most of the better things were retained and went to Oxford. but even so, a partial picture can be drawn. the most immediately noticeable feature was the almost total lack of twentieth-century fiction. I do know that he kept whatever books Christopher Isherwood had inscribed to him with one exception—one of Isherwood's translations of *The Bhagavagad Gita.*

One must also except an immense quantity of paperback "whodunits," obviously his recreational reading. But of serious fiction, again aside from a group presented to him by aspiring nobodies, akin to the poetry presenters mentioned earlier, the only important modern fiction titles were three novels by William Faulkner: *The Town, The Mansion,* and *A Fable.* I guessed that the latter title had attracted his attention due to its religious subject. On the other hand, however, there was quite a large quantity of nineteenth-century novels, particularly Dickens, Trollope and the great Russians.

Commenting on this during our first day of packing he said that Trollope was far superior to Dickens. This led to talk about Victorian prose styles, and eventually he showed me a book which had his favorite "purple passage" in a tome issued as a warning to Victorian young boys about the perils of masturbation. This gave me the opening to ask a question I had long wanted to ask but was too shy to do so, i.e., to ask him to explain the terms "plain sewing" and "hemstitching" which he has used to describe homosexual activities in his review of Ackerley's *My Father and Myself.* He explained that they indicated ventral friction and mutual masturbation, and then continued, "I didn't make them up, you know. But I think I am the first person to use them in print."

I grinned and said, "I suppose that someday you will be credited with the first use of them in some future edition of the *O.E.D.*"

He smiled, obviously pleased, since he had once replied during a television interview when asked if the world were being destroyed and he could save one book, his choice was immediate and hesitating, "Oh, the *O.E.D.,* of course."

He then recalled an anecdote about Thomas Hardy who questioned the meaning of a word unfamiliar to him that had appeared in his daily paper, had gone to the *O.E.D.* for clarification, and was astonished to find himself listed as the first known user of the word.

There was an extremely large quantity of philosophy as well as books dealing with religious dogma and ethics, but surprisingly little on music or the visual arts aside from a badly cannibalized set of the letters of Vincent van Gogh. Following his usual custom when writing reviews, instead of writing out quotations he wished to make in the review, he would tear out the page and paste it onto his review. There was not one single play aside from the Elizabethans who were present in what were obviously his textbooks during his student days at the university. The bulk of the library was, naturally, poetry, including the warned-of books wished off on him by aspiring poets. Of the many hundreds, the only one who seemed to have developed into a major figure was James Fenton, whose first small pamphlet was in the group.

Although Auden would from time to time sell review books that were sent to him by hopeful publishers, he obviously felt that it was *infra dig* to sell anything inscribed to him no matter how unsolicited or unwanted it might be. But there were also, as I had firmly believed there would be, a great deal of very fine and very important material in the form of presentation copies of first editions from such peers as T.S. Eliot, Marianne Moore, C. Day Lewis, Christopher Isherwood, Edmund Wilson, Stephen Spender and Edith Sitwell, to mention only the most famous. Also were present virtually all of his textbooks from his university days, including a long run of Temple Classics. There were also some very astute purchases he had made during that time, including the first English translation of Proust's masterpiece, Laura Riding's first book *A Close Chaplet,* and Ezra Pound's *Quia Pauper Amavi,* all bearing his neat collegiate signature of ownership.

He seems to have abandoned the practice of placing his signature in the books in his libraries as soon as he went down from Oxford, for almost no other book in the whole collection was so marked. This was our only disappointment, for there were a great many books that would have been far more interesting (to say nothing of being far more valuable) had there been any validation that they had been owned and used by Auden. He also rarely annotated anything. In books he was reviewing he generally marked the page numbers he wanted to refer to on the rear end paper, but when one turned to these pages, there appeared marginal scorings opposite certain passages, but no indication of what he thought about the particular passage being cited. The only book that was truly annotated was his Shakespeare, and then only four of the plays. There was also a small volume of ancient Irish poetry that had every blank leaf covered with further specimens he had discovered, all written out in his own hand.

On one of the days when I came across the Shakespeare volume he told be that he had performed in at least two collegian productions, playing Caliban in *The Tempest* and Kate in *The Taming of the Shrew.* What one wouldn't give to have a photograph of him in that role! He came across a volume of limericks, which reminded him of another episode while he was at Oxford, and told me he had known the famous Dr. Spooner. I was astounded, as I had always believed that the man whose name gave rise to "Spoonerisms" had been an early Victorian, but Auden assured me that this was not the case. We all know that Auden has acquired a considerable reputation even during his undergraduate days, and one day while crossing the Common, he was stopped by Dr. Spooner who said to him, "Young man, I want you to come to my rooms next Friday at four to meet W. H. Auden."

The startled Auden replied, "But Dr. Spooner, I *AM* W.H. Auden.

"Never mind, come anyway," said Dr. Spooner, sailing off majestically with his academic robes trailing in his wake, leaving behind him a thoroughly bemused Auden.

The reminiscence and our handling of his books also elicited in him thoughts about his childhood reading, during which we compared our long-ago favorites. When I mentioned *Tom Sawyer* as my own prime favorite juvenile reading, he said that he had had no American books, and missed Mark Twain "as well as that man who wrote about Indians...begins with a 'C'." (James Fenimore Cooper, of course.) This led to a comparison of Christmas customs. As children he and his two older brothers had each written out his wants on slips of paper which were then set afire to float up the chimney. He had, surprisingly, never heard of the American custom of letters to Santa Claus. The conversation then shifted to recent films. At the time Fellini's *The Decameron* and Visconti's *Death in Venice* had been enjoying a considerable vogue. He thought *The Decameron* "Dreadful—after getting through that incredible group of ugly people at the Trimalchian banquet, the rest of the film made no sense whatever. You don't know who is committing suicide, or why."

As to *Death in Venice,* he felt that the distortion of the basic premise of the story—making Tadzio completely aware of his charm—was ruinous, in his words, "Making the boy a cock-tease is all wrong. The man would have groped him immediately. And everyone goes on and on about the beautiful photography. But I've BEEN to Venice!"

He continued, recalling that he used to tease his father-in-law, Thomas Mann, by saying that the only really great modern German writer was Franz Kafka. I asked him if Mann took this in good humor. "Yes, he liked Kafka enough to take it in good form."

Then for some unfathomable reason he showed me some new poems he had written in a peculiar archaic Welsh stanza form, as well as a piece for a *festschrift* in honor of William Empson. He then came across two of the three Oxford pamphlets containing the text of his Latin orations at Oxford in 1958 and 1960, explaining that the only requirement for a poet-in-residence is to make an annual speech in Latin. He also showed me a photograph of graffiti on Oxford walls scrawled by students campaigning for his election to the post. He seemed quite pleased with his popularity among the students. He then switched to describing some on his activities during his wartime service in the Army Air Force, saying that he thought he was probably the first major poet to fly the Atlantic.

Then there was an abrupt change of mood when he told me how indignant he was with Robert Lowell who had just sent him a nasty telegram. It was not until much later that I was able to piece together what had actually happened between them. Auden had told me that he thought Lowell was despicable for circulating mimeographed versions of letters that had passed between him and his second wife, Elizabeth Hardwick. Auden always felt that letters should never be published, even going to the length of leaving instructions to his literary executors to place public notices asking his friends and correspondents to burn his letters. Some did, but fortunately for us, most did not. At any rate, I finally learned that Lowell had used these letters to make the basis of the text for his book entitled *Imitations,* and had sent a mimeographed version prior to the publication of the book itself to several friends, including Auden who had apparently confided his opinion to a mutual friend. Word inevitably got back to Lowell, resulting in the angry telegram.

Then, letting that drop, he remarked that he was trying to give up smoking, but was having no success whatever. All in all, it had been a heady day for me. While every visit with him had been a great treat, this one was far and away the best. He was open and frank, in marvelous good humor, and it also marked for me progress in our friendship. Obviously he now felt that he knew me well enough to go beyond formal politeness and confide in me matters that one does not ordinarily air to casual visitors or strangers.

Among the books he had let me have was one belonging to his partner, Chester Kallman, in fact copy number one of Kallman's first book *Storm at Castelfranco,* containing an original drawing by Larry Rivers. When this failed to show up among the books shipped abroad there had been a domestic crisis. Luckily I had not yet sold it, and when I learned of this through a mutual friend who had been visiting in Austria at the time, I realized that to mail it to Austria would probably be embarrassing to Auden and confirm Chester's worst accusations about Auden selling his possessions. Auden denied having done so and said the book was still safely in the New York apartment. Auden was returning there briefly in the fall.

Shortly thereafter, the last book to be published during his lifetime, *Epistle to a Godson,* had appeared. As always he agreed to let me come over to have it signed, and I was able to return Chester's book by hand. Auden later sent me a note thanking me for this bit of tact. At any rate, while we were chatting, he took *Epistle* and wrote in it. The first time I had gone to his apartment to get books signed, I asked him to inscribe them to me personally. He smiled and said gently, "I've made it a rule to inscribe a person's name only if I know him well, and we haven't known each other long enough for that."

So I never asked again, being content with his usual custom of crossing out his printed name and signing below it. Many years later I learned that this was a rule practiced by T.S. Eliot, and undoubtedly that was the source of Auden's custom. After a short further conversation, during which he accepted my offer to let him stay at my apartment when he returned in the spring for a teaching stint at John Jay College, which was only a few short blocks from my residence, I left. When I returned home I looked into the book and saw that apparently he felt that we knew each other well enough, for he had written,

"For Robert from Wystan."

Alas, I was never to see him again.

Ted Berrigan

Ted Berrigan first came into the shop early on, at the time when he was involved with Lorenz Gude in issuing *C Magazine*. In fact, some of the issues were run off on our mimeo machine (as were also issues of Ed Sanders' notorious and ground-breaking *FUCK YOU/a Magazine of the Arts* and some issues of *The Floating Bear* put out by LeRoi Jones and Diane di Prima.) After that I saw less and less of him. In retrospect I think that this was probably due to the fact that I never displayed any enthusiasm for his work, for I truly did not like it at all, and I think he realized this. I am not sure when he and his first wife, Sandy, divorced, some time in the late 1960s I believe. He then married Alice Notley, and they had two sons. Of course they were always in need of funds. Thus it was Alice who always came into the shop with material for sale, usually correspondence from their peers, or the occasionally inscribed book from one of them. I had a good, friendly relationship with Alice, and always bought everything she offered me for sale. Such was their marginal existence that I always teased Alice about the promptness of her appearance in the shop, saying that the postmarks on the envelopes still had damp ink. Alice always took this in good humor. Although we never discussed poetry, she once remarked that she thought I liked her work better than Ted's. I just smiled. No response was necessary.

Then in the midsummer of 1983 I learned of Ted's sudden death. A memorial service was arranged to take place at the church of St. Marks-in-the-Bouwerie, which for many years had been a venue for poetry readings, especially by the group of poets around Berrigan and Anne Waldman. I felt I should attend, regardless of my opinion of his poetry. I was surprised at the very large turnout. But surprise is hardly the word for my reaction to what I witnessed after I got into the main room of the parish hall—shock is more accurate. There, up on the dais, was an enormous, bigger than life-size nude oil painting of Ted by George Schneeman. It portrayed Ted seated, full frontal, his legs akimbo, displaying his genitalia. I guess I was still a bit old-fashioned in my thinking. I certainly had no problem with nude paintings, but in a church? At a memorial service? Well, whatever. Flanking this portrait were two baskets of flowers, and above it was a traditional crucifix. There was also in front of all this a lectern for the speakers and readers.

The service opened with a young guitarist playing and singing "Abide with Me." This was followed by an extremely shrill soprano massacring "Amazing Grace." It struck me as an extremely odd juxtaposition of the oldest, most trite hymns rendered against the most controversial type of visual art.

Apparently the rector of the church had no problem with this, for he was present and offered a prayer next, which was followed by an ensemble reading of the Ninetieth Psalm. Then Anne Waldman, predictably, was the first of a string of fellow poets either reading or reminiscing, including Reed Bye (then Waldman's husband), Anselmo Hollo, and what I felt was an awkward and graceless speech by Fielding Dawson. Next came Ed Sanders who accompanied himself on a lyre, displaying a rather good singing voice.

In his remarks he also mentioned the magazine *FUCK YOU*. I smiled inwardly, thinking it was probably the first time that those two words had been spoken aloud in an Episcopal church.

The readings and remarks were continued by Kenneth Koch, Anne Waldman again, Andrei Codrescu, and the first Mrs. Berrigan (Sandy). I noticed John Ashbery in the congregation, but he did not speak. Next the guitarist played one of Ted's favorite pop songs, and proceedings were closed with a benediction by the rector.

What happened next seemed weird to me. The large nude portrait was picked up by two of the readers, and a procession of the mourners was formed behind it. It was then carried out the door and around the block, accompanied by a dead march played solemnly on a drum. Passersby on Second Avenue, in this old Polish-Jewish neighborhood, were startled, to say the least.

Creeley, Duncan, and Levertov

P rior to the Beat period, poetry readings were not nearly as common as
they are today. Generally speaking, there were only a few such each
year, even in New York, and usually by the acknowledged giants—
Robert Frost, Marianne Moore, a grudging e.e. cummings, and occasionally transatlantics such as T.S. Eliot and Dylan Thomas. but with the new
audiences who were reading the Beats, the demand for readings by these
new, younger poets changed the scene. However the traditional sponsor and
venue for most of the readings, the Ninety-second Street YMHA apparently took no notice, disdaining these newcomers with a rather haughty "We
don't consider that sort of thing poetry." This was the verbatim answer I
received from Grace Shulman, at the time in charge of the Y's poetry program, when I asked her once why Michael McClure had never been invited
to read under their auspices. And this was well into the late '70s when the
Beat poets had been appearing regularly for several years on university cam-
puses throughout the country.

At any rate, when a triple reading by Denise Levertov, Robert Duncan
and Robert Creeley was announced for April 20, 1964 at the Guggenheim
Museum, the excitement in New York was tremendous. It was sold out the
day the tickets went on sale. Levertov had been living in New York for a
few years then, and had given a couple of readings in small venues. But
Creeley and Duncan had not appeared in New York for several years, and

there had never been a joint reading by these three who were generally regarded as the leading lights of what had become known as the Black Mountain group.(This despite the fact that none of them had actually attended the Black Mountain school in rural North Carolina.) The museum's auditorium, probably the best possible place for such a reading, was attractive and had comfortable seats, perfect sight lines, and superb acoustics. Its only drawback was its relatively small seating capacity. Interest in this reading was intense, and several hundred people had to be turned away.

Levertov was the opener, and made a somewhat lengthy but cogent introduction explaining the close-knit relationship that existed among the trio, and also explained in some detail the effect that the work of the two men had upon her own output. Then Creeley arose to be the first reader. His appearance was striking. He is over six feet tall, rangy and hawk-like. At that time he had a pointed beard so that his appearance conjured up images of D.H. Lawrence. He has only one eye, having lost the left one in a childhood accident. But this solitary eye blazes with an intensity unlike any other I have ever seen. Certainly with this one eye he sees far more and far deeply than most of the rest of us blessed with two eyes. Many years later I was talking with Robert Duncan about Creeley, and asked him if he had the same impression.

"Oh my God, yes! When he reads a book I'm surprised that any print is left on the page," was his reply.

In the beginning few minutes Creeley seemed nervous and constricted, but as I was later to learn, it was not so much nervousness as his inescapable New England heritage, which, indeed, is reflected in his work, which is spare and lean in the extreme. His poems have been surgically pared down to the bone, and beyond. In some of them even the bone has been thinned down to a particularly quivering, living entity that is also paradoxically bone hard and steel strong. He read for approximately twenty minutes. A couple of times he stopped after a few words and announced that he would start over, not having gotten the cadence or the rhythm to his satisfaction, beating time with his right arm to aid in capturing it.

Then he turned the platform over to Levertov, who read with much more assurance and poise than Creeley, which was not that surprising, given the fact that she had made many more platform appearances than he had. I had not attended any of these, having become a fan of her work relatively

Robert Creeley

recently. As soon a I had gathered up everything that had been published by her up to that point, I wrote to her, as was my custom, asking if I might pay a visit in order to get the volumes signed. There hadn't been many demands on her time at that point, so she very kindly suggested an evening for the visit.

Her apartment, where she lived with her husband Mitchell Goodman and their son Nikolai, was located over a meat warehouse on the waterfront in lower Manhattan. Apparently we hit it off, for they accepted my subsequent invitation for dinner at my apartment at the other end of Manhattan in Washington Heights. When they arrived, Denise apologized for not bringing a bottle of wine, saying that they had forgotten that the liquor stores would be closed on Sunday. So instead she brought me the handwritten manuscript of an as-then unpublished poem. I was very happy indeed that the liquor stores were closed.

During the meal I asked many questions, starting with her early life in England. I knew that she had a Welsh mother and a Russian-Jewish father, and wondered why they had given her a French name, "Denise."

"Well," she explained, "there was quite a discussion in the family as to what my name should be, so they put all the name choices in a hat and drew out two of them. So my real first name is Priscilla, and Denise the second. One of the other choices was 'Natalia' which I like better. I think of myself as a Natalia."

When I asked how she had happened to come to the United States, she laughed and replied, "It was to try the ice cream."

Since I looked puzzled she continued, "Well, when Mitch was courting me he told me all about that store—Howard Johnson's is it? Well, the one that has twenty-seven flavors or something. So I married him to be able to taste them all!"

I then switched to bibliographic questions. She was a good listener, something not always true of some of the other poets I have encountered. At any rate, I wanted to know how many copies had been printed of a small pamphlet entitled *Five Poems* published early in her career by the White Rabbit Press in San Francisco. It is actually her third book, and by far the rarest in her entire canon.

"Well, I was coming to San Francisco for a reading at the Poetry Center, and they wanted to have something of mine on sale in the lobby. My first book had been published in England and hadn't been distributed here, and my second, *Here and Now,* was published by Ferlinghetti in his Pocket Poems series, but was already out of print. So Robert Duncan and Jess ran off about two hundred and fifty, certainly not more than three hundred copies of some poems I had sent Robert in letters. They ran them off surreptitiously in the offices of the Greyhound Bus depot, with Robert doing the actual stitching." She added to this that Robert had stabbed himself a few times while sewing the copies, and added with a grin, "Several of them had blood stains. I suppose that would make them 'collector's copies' with the blood of the poet."

Referring again to her early life she said that for several years she had been a full-time ballet student, but one day she realized that she would never be a ballerina and gave up her studies. By this time World War II was in full swing and she served as a volunteer nurse, and at the same time started to write poetry. This led her to tell me that she does not like to let collectors or institutional libraries have her manuscripts, since she works out her poems in her head, sometimes for years, before she commits anything to paper. She feels very strongly that such work sheets would give a totally false impression of her working habits, leading people to assume that she never revised or corrected anything. She said by the time she put anything down on paper, she had "got it" in her head in its finished state.

Towards the end of the evening, I asked her if she knew Margie Cohn, one of the grande dames of the rare book business at the time, and she related her embarrassment when at dinner at Margie's with several other people, the subject of T.S. Eliot came up. Eliot was, according to Margie, one of her closest friends. Without thinking how it sounded, Levertov began her remarks with, "Well, for what he's worth..." or something to that effect.

Denise said that Margie's gasp was audible, and later on when she was showing Denise the apartment, one bedroom was pointed out accompanied by the remark, "Eliot slept here," in such reverential tones, "...just like on the tour when the guide says 'and this was Queen Elizabeth's bed.' "

At the Guggenheim reading Denise's performance did not have the intensity of feeling that Creeley's had, but it was nonetheless superb and evoked applause several times during the reading, something which had not occurred during Creeley's stint. I was rather astonished when she announced that she would read a recent poem of hers entitled *Hypocrite Women.* I had read the poem in a recent poetry journal issued in Greenwich Village and realized that she had used the word "cunt" in it. Nowadays that wouldn't cause the slightest ripple, but this was in the early '60s before such words were used in print, let alone spoken aloud in a public forum such as this reading. The listeners were totally silent for a few seconds when she had concluded the poem, but then there were fervent bursts of applause from scattered portions of the audience.

Then Robert Duncan arose and took the platform. Of the three, he was the consummate showman. He obviously delighted in being before an audience and played to it like the superb actor that he was. He read, among other things, a long poem in tribute to Hilda Doolittle, his most important master. By general consensus, this was the high point of the entire evening. His mind, as always, ran faster than his ability to speak the word aloud, and he interrupted his poems to give us parenthetical remarks or explanations, sometimes continuing on without completing a thought or a phrase. I was later to learn that his was typical of his ordinary day-to-day conversational style. He always assumed that his listeners were familiar enough with his frames of reference so that there was no need to complete totally any statement. He would give you the gist and you were supposed to be able to pick up the train of thought, finish it rapidly in your mind, and permit him to get on with the next part of his discourse.

He was also given to wild bits of comedy, with a shrewd and telling wit. but strangely, he became nervous while reading his H.D. poem, so much that he tore the pages loose from the binder from which he was reading, holding the detached sheets with both hands which shook visibly and violently. But oddly, his voice and delivery were so smooth that had we been able to see only his face, no one could have had any inkling of the inner storm which was raging.

After the reading had concluded, there was a crush of people onto the stage to get books signed. I spoke briefly to Margie Cohn and Frances Steloff, the two rival grande dames of the book word, who had both attended, something they rarely did, testifying to the uniqueness of the event. Then I joined the mob on stage to get two books signed for my personal collection. Duncan had also agreed to let me publish a broadside poem. At the time I had just formed the idea of issuing a series of such, but it became apparent to me, at least, that broadsides were springing up like mushrooms after a rain, ant that there were far too many of them already on the market. I tried to speak to Creeley but he was so engulfed in admirers that it was physically impossible to get near him.

By this time the museum attendants were turning out the lights so they could close up. I turned to Denise to let her know that I had showed up, since she had personally invited me. She whispered in my ear that there was to be a party afterwards at her home. I went out of the building with Lowell Cohen, one of my customers who was also a fan of Creeley, who had driven me uptown in his car. We stopped briefly at his apartment for a quick bite of food and also to pick up some more books from his collection to get signed, figuring it would not be quite so hectic at the party.

It was in full swing when we arrived. Looking back now it seems that virtually every younger poet then in New York was there—the hostess Levertov, of course, plus Duncan, Ed Sanders, John Wieners, Wendell Berry, Galway Kinnell, LeRoi Jones (later to become Amiri Baraka), Robert Kelly, Paul Blackburn, Allen Ginsberg, and Peter Orlovsky among others whom I have undoubtedly forgotten. For some reason never explained, Creeley did not attend. I was pleasantly surprised by the attention given me as the publisher of Wieners' *Ace of Pentacles.* The depth of respect among his peers for Wieners' work truly surprised me.

From the vantage point of three ensuing decades, it is now plain that this volume contains his best work. I had felt its power when I first read the manuscript, but had no real knowledge of how widespread the admiration for his work was. The party did not start to break up until three a.m. I left with a group consisting of LeRoi Jones and his wife Hettie, Allen Ginsberg, Peter Orlovsky and Ed Sanders, all riding the subway uptown. It's hard to believe nowadays that it was perfectly safe to use the subways then at that late and lonely hour of the morning.

The next evening the party seemed to continue at the Phoenix, with a large group of the previous night's attendees converging on my shop; this time Robert Kelly and his wife Jobyna, Denise and her husband Mitch Goodman, Barbara Joseph, John Wieners, Gerard Malanga and Robert Duncan. Over tea and cookies the conversation continued until two a.m. Everyone then left except Robert Duncan, who told me that he wanted to come see my Gertrude Stein collection. Of course I was charmed by this, and suggested that he come up in the morning. But no, to my amazement he wanted to come up immediately, then and there. It was now well after two a.m., and I lived at 157th Street and Riverside Drive, a one-hour ride once the subway came along. And at that wee hour of the morning that happened only three times an hour. But Duncan was insistent, so off we went. I later learned that there was a bit of deviousness in all this. On the way I gleaned a lot of important and valuable bibliographic data about his early publications.

Once safely in my apartment we looked at all the Stein first editions I possessed—not a lot at this time, but apparently several things that Duncan had never seen before. He then totally astounded me by asking if I had any pornographic photos he could look at. Then, seeing the astonishment in my face, he began unfolding extremely intimate details of his own early sexual history—all this at something like five a.m., after a long, long day! He persisted, saying that it all started when he was fifteen years old, when he followed a "toughie" into a secluded section of a park near his home, but took fright and began to run away. The toughie pursued him and eventually caught him, whereupon he started beating Duncan up, using brass knuckles, so severely that the flesh was torn away from his lower jaw. His screams attracted the police who were only four blocks away. He then said that for some strange feeling of *noblesse oblige* he refused to give any information as to the identity of his assailant.

At the age of twenty-one he came to New York, penniless as his allowance had been cut off because of his refusal to take over the management of the family's architectural firm. He became a hustler, not out of greed, but as he put it, "To make my room for the night." He went on to elaborate on the life of a hustler. The ideal evening was to find a Scarsdale or Westchester husband who wanted a quick, anonymous fling before returning home to the wife and kids, and who would rent a hotel room in which you could spend the remainder of the night. He also explained, "If you haven't made it by ten p.m., you knew you would have to perform all night with whomever and whatever you could pick up.

Some time later he became a kept boy for a French professor at the University of Delaware, who kept him discreetly and at some safe distance in Philadelphia. But then the professor transferred to St. John's College in Annapolis, Maryland, far too small a town to disguise such a liaison. so once again Duncan was kept at a safe distance, this time in a hotel room in

Baltimore, where Duncan became bored beyond endurance. One day he slipped away, going back to New York, and once more was being kept, this time by one of the Mafiosi. Every time Duncan went anywhere he was followed and his every activity reported in detail to his paramour. This became too much for Robert, so one day he successfully eluded his shadower, simply disappeared without a trace, and lived in the mid-West in total obscurity. It was here that he married, but it was not a success, and he eventually was divorced. During this period he started getting poems published and felt that it was safe to live openly once again. He moved to San Francisco where he teamed up with Jess Collins, a painter, who always preferred to be known by his Christian name alone. They lived together until Duncan's death in 1988.

Robert also laughingly told me about a seminar at which he, Jess and W.H. Auden were all housed in one hotel room. Jess managed to get some sleep, but Auden wanted to have sex with Duncan, who decided to acquiesce so they could get it over with and get some sleep. but according to Duncan,

Robert Duncan circa 1965, chez Robert Wilson

despite his continual struggles, Auden could not achieve orgasm, but refused to give up until almost dawn—as it was by the time this narration had been completed.

The next morning, after only a few hours sleep, Duncan asked if he could remain *chez moi* for the remainder of his stay in New York. Before arriving in New York he had accepted Diane di Prima's offer of hospitality, but after the first night he was too uncomfortable to continue staying there. Diane was, of course, generous to a fault and could not refuse help to anyone who asked for it. This resulted in a large number of adults and children coming and going at all hours, so that time or space for thinking out one's program for the day, or doing any writing whatever, were simply not available. So I gladly agreed. Duncan then went happily off on his errands while I went off to Brooklyn on my first visit to Louis Zukovsky, which will be discussed further on,

That day I closed the shop early to attend another poetry reading by Creeley, who wanted to give a "private" reading where "he would know all the faces." Apparently he was not satisfied with his performance at the Guggenheim. so in a very run-down theater at 145 Bleecker Street which Diane di Prima was using for her "Poet's Theater," he gave a magnificent performance, sitting on the remains of a bare stage with only a broken table, for an audience of approximately seventy-five close friends and fellow poets, including all of the attendees at Levertov's party plus Gregory Corso.

It was more like a running conversation than a reading, with Creeley reminiscing for long stretches about personal events in his life that led to the writing of certain poems, which he would them read to us. One included a wildly comic episode when he was living in Provence near Levertov and her husband Mitch. They were sitting in the first row and kept adding details to the story. Creeley's wonderful, genuine laughter got virtually out of control, as did Levertov's and of course, by then, that of most of the audience. It was like a wonderful family gathering. But here again, just as at the Guggenheim reading, he kept beating time in the air, and also once again here, would stop and start all over again when he hadn't gotten the rhythm he wanted. This helped considerably, since his rhythms are not the ordinary ones encountered in most poetry. He ended the evening by reading a chapter from his novel *The Island*. I had read this work, but was now amazed at the intense musicality and poetic quality of the prose which had eluded me during my reading of it, but which was now abundantly clear.

In talking with Creeley afterwards he twice mentioned John Wieners' "unembarrassed grace" and said that he would like to have me publish a book of his similar to that of Wieners'. In the event, this did not happen, sorry to say. The financial situation of the Phoenix had been extended to

Robert Wilson and Robert Duncan, Sautens, Austria

its absolute limit by John's book. By the time we were able to consider such a project, Creeley's reputation had grown so much that other mainstream publishers were offering him far more generous terms than I could afford, so it never came to fruition, to my undying regret.

After the reading we went through the pouring rain to Diane di Prima's place. Having virtually no income, she was nevertheless the provider for a large miscellany of children, various ex-lovers, her current (and third) husband along with his current male lover, and assorted hangers-on. She had invaded a boarded-up condemned building facing the Cooper Union building in the area that was to become known as the East Village. We had to sneak through a removable portion of the nailed-up door, stumble up an unlighted stairway (a light would have betrayed the squatters to the authorities) to the next floor. It was more or less a shambles, with her oldest child asleep on the floor, oblivious to the party going on around her. I could see at once why Robert Duncan had asked to stay at my apartment. I went home fairly early, exhausted after the marathon of three days of intense saturation in poetry and poets.

On a subsequent visit to New York, Duncan was again staying with me and wanted to visit a large exhibition of the Pre-Raphaelite painters on view at the short-lived Huntington Hartford Museum in Columbus Circle. We were accompanied by his longtime friend and colleague, the elfin Helen Adam, who still retained her charming Scots accent. When we reached the final gallery, we were all enchanted and decided to go back and go through the exhibition once more. I suggested that we play a game that I had invented, to wit, if you were in a room and someone yelled "Fire!" which painting would you grab? They were both delighted with this idea and off we went. Now I should mention that the barrel-chested Robert Duncan's voice was resonant and booming, and we progressed through the museum with his "I'll take this one!" being very audible. We were vastly amused to see that pretty soon we were being followed by a guard who, in one gallery filled with heroic sized Burne-Jones paintings of the medusa legend, was actually counting the paintings as we exited the room!

A few years later I made a second visit to California and asked if I might stay with Robert and Jess. Robert was a long time answering, finally extending the invitation, accompanied by a long list of prohibitions, none of which struck me as having been necessary even to mention. Robert eventually explained that they almost never had guests, since it interrupted Jess' routine too much. This was their second residence, but at last both Jess with the success of his paintings and Robert with his royalties increasing had been able to purchase it and make such alterations as pleased them. Robert had one entire floor to house his books, Jess had most of another floor for his atelier, and there was the luxury of a spare room in which I slept. They had renovated the rear portion of the house by adding a second staircase, the walls of which were pierced with several windows to make use of some Victorian stained glass panes which they had rescued from a condemned building nearby. There was a great deal of bric-a-brac and several very fine Tiffany lamps. All this was guarded by two large cats, one very friendly white one named Tommy and a sleek glossy black named Orlando. As Robert explained, "We called him Orlando because as a kitten we weren't sure of his sex, and we had made so many mistakes with previous cats."

While I never made another trip to California, Robert came to New York from time to time, sometimes staying with me, sometimes not. The last visit with him was not in New York, but in Austria, where my good friend Kenneth Doubrava and I were spending some weeks in the Ötztal portion of the Tyrol, in a huge, ancient house belonging to our painter friend Nell Blaine. It was situated in a hamlet high up, which clung to the mountainside and consisted of four houses, an inn and a tiny church that was in operation only one Sunday out of the month. Robert was that year lecturing in Austria in the nearby city of Innsbruck at the same time we were in residence. So it was arranged that he would come for a visit one weekend.

It was a delightful time, with Robert at his garrulous, discursive, witty best. A lot of it was literary gossip, filling us in with such tidbits as Denise Levertov's unrequited love for Robert Creeley, as well as his sadness that he and Levertov were now estranged after more than three decades of close friendship. She had taken umbrage when he wrote in a letter that he liked her most recent book very much because she had gotten back her lovely, lyrical tone. She took this to imply that her anti-Vietnam poems had not been good. It was an opinion that many critics shared, as did I as well. Some of his other gossip, juicy and delightful as it was, simply cannot be committed to the printed page since it concerned poets who are still very much alive.

I was also charmed to discover that Robert shared with us a passion for gathering wild mushrooms, which was one of our main reasons for coming to Austria at this time of year, the height of the tourist season. Although I did not know it at the time, it was the last time I was to see Robert. So my final memory of him is his great delight that evening in a meal that Kenneth prepared consisting solely of various sautéed mushrooms, including the highly treasured chanterelles that we had gathered on our rambles that afternoon.

Diane di Prima

The poet with whom I have the most enduring friendship is Diane di Prima. We met almost as soon s I took over the Phoenix. She had worked there off and on with the previous owner, Larry Wallrich, and had a proprietary feeling about the shop. One of the few female members of the Beat group, she is undoubtedly the most tirelessly active poet of either sex. She was living at the time with her third husband, Alan Marlowe, in a condemned building—quite illegally, of course—in what is now called the East Village. Actually it was on Cooper Union Square, just a few houses south of the Cooper Union Building, among whose claims to fame is that it was the locale for the one of Abraham Lincoln's campaign speeches that really brought him to national prominence. Diane was there not only with her husband, but her three children from prior attachments, as well as an enormous number of hangers-on, musicians, poets, various ex-lovers of her bisexual husband, and all too often, simply spongers. Virtually none of them had jobs or could in any way contribute money to the communal establishment, but somehow Diane always managed to supply food and shelter for anyone who came knocking at her door.

At that time LeRoi Jones (who had not yet become Amiri Baraka) also lived in the building with his wife Hettie and their three children. Diane and LeRoi were then jointly editing and publishing one of the seminal Beat magazines, *The Floating Bear*. With virtually no funds, it was a plain, no-nonsense journal, consisting of mimeographed pages, with no covers until the very last few issues, stapled together and mailed to a select list of friends

Diane di Prima with her husband Alan Marlowe (right)
and his "husband" John Braden (left)

and the rare subscriber. This joint effort led to an unexpected "special issue," a daughter who is now very successful in the music world.

In order to support this large and often changing menage, Diane quite often came into the shop with items to sell—books sent to her by other poets, correspondence from them, sometimes a mimeographed product, usually one of her own plays. It was one of these that caused the only argument we ever had. I bought some of them, and managed to sell a few, mainly to university libraries which relied on me to keep them abreast of just such esoteric publications from the Beat World. A month or two later

Diane appeared one evening with even more copies, now with a stiff pictorial cover, stating that these were the 'deluxe' edition. I balked: I didn't think that I'd be able to sell any more copies, and I didn't want to jeopardize my relationship with the university libraries by trying to sell them something that was patently and simply a way to make more money. This was early in my tenure at the shop, and we were living a hand-to-mouth existence, barely managing to cover our monthly expenses. I had to be careful with what little money was coming in. Diane was disappointed and angry, and as she stormed out she called back from the door, "I don't know how you run this business."

And in just as much anger, I retorted, "Well, I DO know how you run yours." Luckily we both survived this outburst of tempers, and have remained friends over the ensuing decades.

Diane has never made a secret of the fact that early on she had a Lesbian relationship during her college days. She once told me, with many laughs about it, of an experience when she was waiting in a Greenwich Village hangout much favored by Lesbians. A sailor wandered in, innocent of the reputation of the bar, and was trying to pick up a date. Diane was watching with much amusement at his lack of success with the female patrons. One in particular got up and walked out. He then came over and sat down by Diane, lamenting, "She likes girls."

Diane shrugged her shoulders. What was there to be said? The sailor seemed stunned. Finally, deciding to try again, he asked Diane if she liked girls. She replied truthfully, "Sometimes."

It took the sailor some time in his slightly alcoholic condition to process this reply. Finally something clicked, and he snapped out of his reverie and said, "Come on. Let's go out and find some girls."

Another time she told me of an impromptu menage-a trois episode in which she was the third part of a triangle, the other two participants being Allen Ginsberg and Jack Kerouac. Ginsberg was totally homosexual, and very much in love with Kerouac, who was primarily heterosexual. He would occasionally allow himself to be trade with Allen, but really preferred to bed females. On this occasion he agreed to Allen's importuning, but only if it would be a three-way affair. Diane willingly agreed to the idea. She didn't go into lascivious details about who did what, with which, and to whom. but she did say that it went on all night. Ah, the stamina of youth!

Diane di Prima

Robert Wilson and Diane di Prima

However, after a while, as she told me, she began to feel that she wanted children, and when she found herself pregnant she was happy with the idea and subsequently discontinued her free and easy style of life. By the time I got to know her she had already had two daughters by two different fathers. Ultimately she would have five children, three daughters and two sons, all now grown, and at least two grandchildren. Even though I have known Diane nearly four decades, it is difficult to picture her as a grandmother. This is somewhat strange for me, because she is the perfect "Earth Mother" type, welcoming anyone who needs care, support, mothering. Her expansive nature seems to thrive on the opportunity to be the provider.

At times, after the condemned building on Cooper Square was no longer available, she rented a very large room at the Hotel Albert in the

Village. Lord knows how many people were living there at one time. It was difficult to count, as the various residents showed up at all hours, reminding me of the Windmill Theatre in London during the Blitz, with its motto "We Never Closed." Diane's door was never closed, it seemed. And regardless of how scarce money was, large, filling meals, usually soups or stews but nonetheless nourishing, were somehow provided for the whole motley crew.

While I was never penniless, I was quite often in need of a shoulder to lean on, especially when my latest romance had fizzled out and I was plunged into gloom. Diane was always there to jolly me out of it. And once Diane accepted you into her circle, it was for keeps. Which is why, now nearly forty years after our first meeting, we are still intimate friends, even though we seldom see each other because of the spatial difficulties between the two coasts. But ours is the most enduring of all my literary friendships. And it also seems that a joking remark by Alan Marlowe, her third husband, may just come true

I was at my desk, and Diane was sitting beside it while we were negotiating some business, probably the sale of some books and letters. Alan was much amused by the process, and said that thirty or forty years into the future, there we would be, looking like Marianne Moore and Ezra Pound. We laughed, of course, but the more I think of it, the more accurate it may prove to be. We are both survivors, and even though I am a generation older than Diane, I intend to be around when her red hair, like Marianne's famous red, has turned to snow white, so that I will be able to repeat to Diane Ezra's line to Marianne—"You are an old man's darling."

Faulkner on Fire Island

No, as far as anyone knows, William Faulkner never set foot on Fire Island. This is, rather, the story of how the long-lost manuscript of his first novel *Soldier's Pay* was found by me on Fire Island in the late 1960s.

For several years I had been spending a large part of each summer on this carefree, sun-drenched idyllic sand spit. Reasonably accessible from New York, (except on Friday afternoons in midsummer), it is a couple of miles off the south shore of Long Island, with about a dozen communities at intervals on its forty-mile length. It is completely unspoiled, no roads, no commercial establishments other than a grocery store and a liquor store in some of the settlements, making it a great restorative from the tensions of urban life. with none of the so-called "conveniences" of modern city life, There is nothing to do but bask in the sun on one of the most glorious beaches in the world during the day, and go to dinners and parties or to the disco dance palace in the evening. By four p.m., the sun is beginning to get too low in the sky to do any further suntanning, and it is customary to sit on one's deck and have pre-dinner cocktails, often with friends or neighbors. On one such occasion I was sitting with an elderly man who had been both friend and neighbor for the past several years. Somewhere between drinks, he said, "Bob, I understand you have a bookshop."

"Yes, Louie, didn't you know?"

"No, I never did. Tell me, is Faulkner worth anything?"

Instantly my guard went up. Countless are the times that I have been asked such a question by hopeful but uninformed owners of dog-eared book club editions, or Modern Library books, or other such usually worthless specimens. And in addition to this, I knew Louie to be from New Orleans, and even if the books were first editions, every book that I have ever seen that came out of New Orleans has been so badly foxed or mildewed that it was hopeless as a collector's copy.

But Louie was a friend, so I had to be polite and try to let him down gently, and anyway, who knew what he might have. Little did I suspect the magnitude of what he actually possessed. So playing it close to the vest, I replied, "Well, it all depends."

"Bill and I were roommates after the war, you know."

(No, I hadn't known—and surprise number two was hearing him call Faulkner "Bill.") I had never known Louie to be a name-dropper or to presume familiarity of this sort if it were not entirely true. My interest perked up considerably.

He continued, "When he decided to get married, we split up, and he let me keep the manuscript of his first book."

("My God, the manuscript of *The Marble Faun!*" I thought.) Putting my drink down on the deck, I sat as erect as one can in a canvas beach chair.

"You mean *The Marble Faun?*" I demanded.

"No, no, that's not the title. I mean his first novel." ("Better yet," thought I.)

"Where is it, Louie?"

"Back at the house, somewhere."

I stood up quickly. "Come on, let's go," I said as I tried to pull him up out of his chair.

"No, no, not now. I'll have to look for it tonight, and I'll bring it over tomorrow if I can find it. Then he took another sip of his drink.

I knew him well enough to know that it was useless to try to push him when he said no, but also well enough to know that if he promised something, he kept his word to a tee, like the true Southern Gentleman of the old school that he was.

All the next day I fidgeted on the beach, returning to the house five or six times to see if perhaps Louie had come by and left a note. No such luck. But finally, after the usual late supper, down the walk he came with a large cardboard shirt box under his arm. When he put it sown on the table my heart was pounding even faster, for it was the original mailing carton addressed to Faulkner with Phil Stone's return address in the corner. Stone, of course, had been Faulkners friend and agent, and had been responsible for getting the novel published. And the whole thing was authenticated by the stamps of the period, and a clearly legible 1926 postmark.

Feeling in some degree the way Howard Carter must have felt when he broke the seal on King Tutankhamen's tomb, I lifted the lid. There was an enormous pile of legal size typed paper, perhaps five hundred or more pages. But then my heart sank, for the top page was headed "Chapter Five."

"Damn," I thought, "It's only part of the manuscript." Even while thinking this my fingers were digging down at the corner of the box to lift the entire pile out. When I had gotten all the papers out, I started riffling through them, and very quickly saw that there was more than the novel, or even merely part of it, for there suddenly came to light a sheaf of hand written poems in Faulkner's unmistakable minuscule handwriting. Further along were some typed pages from a different ribbon, black, whereas the novel had been typed on a purple ribbon.

"Well, what do you think? Is it worth anything?"

"I'm not sure whether the entire book is here, Louie. It starts at Chapter Five, and it may be only part of the book. But there are some poems and maybe some short stories. It'll take a while to sort it out before I can be sure. But it is worth a lot no matter how it turns out."

"Well, why don't you take it to the shop and call me next week."

Which of course is exactly what I did. It was only then that I discovered the magnitude of the cache. My fears about it being only part of *Soldier's Pay* were soon dispelled. The pages simply had gotten mixed up at some time over the intervening years since the carton came into Louie's possession, and not only was it the entire book, it was there doubled in spades, so to speak, for present was an alternative ending never published, and of course until then, totally unknown. There were thirteen poems in holograph, of which seven were unpublished, as well as fifteen short stories with three of them both unpublished and unknown until then. And, finally, the typescript of an early book review by Faulkner.

The following Tuesday I telephoned Louie at home as promised. The phone rang for some time and just as I was on the verge of hanging up, he answered. When he heard my voice he immediately asked, "Well, what's the verdict?"

"Are you sitting down?" I countered.

"Yes, I am," he replied, and before I could say anything he continued, "Do you think I can get enough out of it to take a trip to Portugal?"

"Louie, you can buy Portugal!"

Which is very nearly what he did. For Louie, having reached mandatory retirement age that year, took the proceeds, went to Portugal and bought a house there in which he resided happily for the rest of his life. He lived a completely happy life there, thanks to his foresight in saving the manuscript of a then totally unknown writer.

There was, of course, no trouble in disposing of this truly unbelievable find. I first telephoned Lola Szladits, then the head of the prestigious Berg Collection of British and American Literature, situated within the New York Public Library. I always alerted Lola to any gems that came my way, since she needed time to get authorization for the expenditure of large sums.

Her reply was instantaneous, "Of course we want it. It's the last lion not in captivity."

This came into my hands just at the time I was preparing our one-hundredth catalog, a number that seemed to call for more than the usual run of offerings. I had been hoarding "goodies" for some time for this purpose. Obviously this would be the star attraction. And indeed it seemed the entire East Coast of the United States wanted it. As soon as the catalog was in the mails, we received telephone orders from the University of Maryland, the University of Virginia (which was particularly nettled that I had not offered it to then in advance, since Faulkner had given them the manuscripts of all his other novels,) the University of North Carolina and the University of Georgia. Strangely enough, the University of Mississippi remained silent.

But Virginia was far from silent. Shortly after I had to tell them on the telephone that the manuscript had already been sold, I received a letter from Faulkner's publishers advising me that in their opinion, I had violated copyright laws by using a portion of one page of the manuscript as an illustration in my catalog. Obviously, the University of Virginia had alerted them to the catalog appearance. I replied, reminding them that such usage was, in fact, allowable under the current copyright laws, and had been common practice for a great many years. A letter also arrived from the librarian at the University of Virginia in the same mail taking me to task for not offering them the manuscript first, especially since they were the owners of all of Faulkner's other manuscripts, and therefor this one should rightly, in their opinion, come to them.

My reply to them was that while this was true, a book store had to think about which customers were frequent purchasers, and that while I had been sending my catalogs to them for nearly a decade, they had purchased exactly two books for slightly over one hundred dollars in all that time. Not exactly what you would call ongoing support. There was, naturally, no reply to this letter. But I was vastly amused when the next catalog appeared, for an order for several dozen titles arrived from Virginia. Obviously my reply had made an impact. But of course, there were no more lions for me to capture for them, so after that there was no contact between us.

Jean Garrigue

In the early days on Cornelia Street a young woman, slender, rather shy and soft-spoken, came in quite often looking for some of the more obscure publications of Marianne Moore. Since Moore was one of my favorite poets, and one with whom I had enjoyed a warm relationship for several years, I was able to offer not only some of the books, but also bits of information and suggestions. I mentioning that she should try to obtain a copy of the New York Public Library's pamphlet on Moore, which contained the only bibliography of her at that time. She thanked me, but returned a few days later to report that not only was it long out of print, but that the library could not locate their own reference copy.

This came as no surprise to me, for that was the same report I was given fifty percent of the time when I attempted to do research there. She then asked of she might borrow my copy. this put me in a considerable quandary. A book shop isn't a lending library, especially when it concerns its own irreplaceable reference books. But something made me break my own rule. So I handed it to her and asked her to give me her name and address or telephone number in case I needed it before she returned it. I was more than astonished when she wrote "Jean Garrigue" on the piece of paper I handed her.

I had collected her works before taking over the Phoenix, and was more than pleased that I had agreed to help her. It then turned out that she was writing a monograph about Moore for the University of Minnesota's ongoing series of pamphlets on major American writers. Despite the slender size of this treatise, it remains to this day the best treatment of Moore yet published, at least in my opinion.

I don't know if my surprise showed when I read the name on the paper as she returned it to me, but I do recall verbatim bursting out with, "Oh my God! Why didn't you tell me before who you are? You are one of my favorite poets," which I think truly embarrassed her. From then on, the tone of her visits were decidedly less formal.

In addition to asking her to sign my copies of her books, I once requested that she write something in the shop's guest book. Unwittingly my request came hard upon the heels of the death of her favorite cat, for she wrote a poignant tribute to it ending with an afterthought hoping I would never have to suffer a similar loss of either of the two white cats who helped me run the shop.

Jean was a figure of contrasts. Much of the time she would be a quiet, shy figure. But when with friends she could trust, she would blossom into a high-spirited, fun-loving creature, more than willing to try anything, at least once. a lot of this seemingly carefree attitude was a mask to cover her basic insecurity. As with almost all poets, she was never sure that her work was what she felt it ought to be. I've always felt that she was one of the several superb, first-rate poets who never seemed to win the public recognition they deserved. She was a serious, dedicated craftsman, truly inspired, and she has also added to that small portion of work that will endure, as T.S. Eliot once so famously wrote of Marianne Moore, Jean's own source of inspiration.

Just about the time that the shop moved over to Jones Street, Jean left New York and moved to Boston, so I did not see her during the last few years of her life. he died rather young, alas for all of us. She never made much money from her poetry, and oftimes was hard put to buy the books she wanted or needed. Quite often she would come in with copies of her own books, plaintively asking if I could take them in trade for whatever it was that she needed. I was always happy to do so, for I never had to keep them in stock for very long. There were enough poetry lovers who knew of her excellence, even if she was unaware of their existence.

Rider Haggard's "She"

During the early part of the '70s, one of the Phoenix's customers who had formed an impressive collection of the works of Henry Miller had reached that deadly stage—nothing more existed to add to the collection. He decided to sell it and asked me to fly down to Florida to look at it. This was midwinter, so an excuse to go to Florida was very welcome. I did go through the enormous collection which filled nine large cartons, and agreed on a price. Then the owner surprised me by offering a second collection of the novels of that very prolific Victorian author, H. Rider Haggard.

The collection was extensive, although not totally complete. I turned it down at the time, since the Phoenix had up to that time never dealt in anything other than twentieth-century literature. But during the flight back, I began to think more about it, since Haggard's two most famous works—*King Solomon's Mines* and *She,* especially the latter—had provided me with one of the most fascinating experiences of my life.

Rarely, if ever, is anyone privileged to meet the actual heroine of a work of fiction, especially from the Victorian era. But that is precisely what happened to me in 1949, when I was stationed in Pretoria with the American embassy. I had not been there very long before I began to hear stories that at first I discounted, but eventually concluded that they were based on fact. Rider Haggard's famous *She* had not only been based on an actual woman, but this very same woman was still alive, very elderly of course, but nonetheless actually existing. and even more amazing was the fact that the basic outline of his plot was hardly fictionalized at all, but was, rather, an accurate rendering of local beliefs and legends attached to Queen Modjadji, for such was her actual name.

I became, of course, inordinately curious, and after many inquiries, finally made the acquaintance of Geoff Lombard, a young ethnology student at the University of Pretoria. He not only confirmed the stories, but generously offered to take me along on an expedition with four other students who hoped to visit the legendary "She." So with bedrolls, cameras, brandy, a pistol, enough food for a week, and the usual heap of camping equipment, the six of us set out.

The first day's drive was uneventful, but the scenery began to be more interesting after we crossed the Tropic of Capricorn just north of the old Boer city of Pietersburg. The land was barren and rocky, dotted here and there with native huts or 'kraals", and a few euphorbia trees, which resemble giant cacti more than trees. Off in the distance were mountains of singular beauty, part of the Drakensburg Range. Lombard pointed out individual mountains, all with picturesque names, one pair of twin peaks being engagingly and unforgettably known as "Sheba's Breasts."

A light rain continued throughout the next day, but failed to deter us. Shortly after lunch we arrived at Duivelskloof where the real obstacle had to be hurdled. It was necessary to obtain from the commissioner of native affairs a permit to enter the native reserve area. Lombard had written in advance from the university requesting such. Our luck was good, for the commissioner was in an affable mood, and had even gone so far as to send a message to the queen's village that a group of white visitors would have permission to visit her capital soon. This guaranteed us only entrance into the reserve area. While the commissioner could grant us permission to see the queen, he could not force her to admit us to the royal presence.

Thus armed with official sanction, we proceeded out of the town on a fairly smooth dirt road, following the commissioner's instructions as far as we could. Then we had to resort to asking directions from natives along the way. After a few fruitless queries, we were finally directed to a rough path, deeply rutted with rain gullies, which led almost straight up the side of the mountain foothills. The car at times almost failed to make the grade, but after a good bit of slipping and skidding, we arrived at a relatively flat space under a giant morella tree, behind which was a primitive high pole fence. The native grapevine had apparently functioned more efficiently than our automobile, for an official delegation, consisting of the head man of the tribe and the queen's "secretary of state" were under the tree to greet us. After introductions, which to my surprise were held in English, we entered the village. The secretary of state, (with whom we became familiar enough with to call by his Christian name, Donald) was dressed in an old cotton shirt and faded denim trousers. He apologized for the lack of ceremony, explaining that we had not been expected until the next day, and hoped that we would not be disappointed that no preparations had been made for us. This pleased rather than disappointed us, for we would undoubtedly get thereby a truer picture of native life than if a special reception had been provided.

We had successfully passed the first two hurdles, and now remained the supreme question. Would the all-powerful, eternal "She" grant us a glimpse of herself? Lombard finally managed to ask Donald if the queen would receive us. Donald, like a true diplomat, declined to commit himself, but agreed to transmit our request. While we awaited Donald's return, Lombard told us all that he had been able to gather concerning Modjadji, both fact and fiction. She was indeed Rider Haggard's inspiration for "She", and was the reigning queen of the Lovedu tribe. But here fact soon became inextricably mingled with fiction, superstition and legend.

Modjadji still reigns as ruler of the Lovedu tribe of the Bantu people. (Since this encounter took place in 1949, the one I met and am describing has died, as has her successor, so that now a putative granddaughter is the reigning "Modjadji.") According to native belief she is eternal, just as she was in Rider Haggard's novel. Native belief also attributes to her the control of the rain, by virtue of her being the mother of the sun. She can, accordingly, cause her offspring to come and go as she wills, and thereby release or withhold rain. It is this control of the all-important life-giving rain in an otherwise desert country which gives her both her spiritual and her political power. The technical side of rain-making has been neatly solved by Modjadji in locating her capital on the rim of the first mountains that break the plains extending inland from the Indian Ocean coast. Rain-bearing clouds hit the "Modjadji" area and give up their water content. although her political territory is relatively small, and her tribe not at all numerous, her religious sway as the Rain Queen extends over the entire lower portion of the African continent. In times of drought, natives from as far away as Cape Town, almost fifteen hundred miles distant, have been known to send herds of cattle to her in supplication not to withhold the rain.

Modjadji's seemingly eternal life was explained to us by Mr. Mothivi, an educated, intelligent member of the tribe, who had returned to his native village as a school teacher. The queen possesses, as far as the native populace believes, the power to rejuvenate herself at certain intervals. She accomplished this just as Haggard's "She" does, by going into a cave in the mountains, and after a few days, emerging as a young girl once more. There have been two "rejuvenations" within recorded history, and the third is now overdue. The incumbent, the first to receive white visitors, has a reluctance to "rejuvenate" herself, since according to the secret tribal ritual, she must commit suicide in the cave by drinking poison. A young relative, usually a daughter or granddaughter, who has been reared secretly by the tribal elders, is then brought forth as the rejuvenated queen.

As far as historians can gather, the first two queens were white. There are one or two accounts of reliable persons who saw the second Modjadji before the Boer War, who maintained that her skin was white, and that she had blue eyes and blonde hair, precluding the possibility of her being an albino. The best explanation put forward to date is that the first queen was probably the survivor of a group of Voortrekkers who were massacred in the 1840s. This child was supposedly raised by a local witch doctor who eventually got her accepted as the tribal head when the contemporary king died without an heir.

When Donald came back he told us that although the queen had not expected us, she would receive us immediately; there was a royal "beer party" in progress which we were to join. A beer party is not as innocuous as it sounds. Kaffir beer is quite a bit more potent than the product with which most Americans are familiar. It is far closer to hillbilly "moonshine," being a distillation of fermented corn and yeast, yielding a thick, milky, and extremely powerful beverage. Aside from being a social stimulant, beer is one of the three forms of money, cattle and wives being the other two. This particular beer party was no small everyday affair, but was to celebrate the queen's betrothal to another "bride." We were surprised to learn that the queen married "wives," and upon inquiry found out that she had not only married wives, but also maintained a harem, the members of which were her servants. The basic reason for this harem is its role in the complicated system of keeping the tribal economy stabilized. Cattle and wives are the two most important types of money. In fact, a wife can be procured only by purchasing her with cattle. The queen, in her position of head of the tribe, is traditionally duty-bound to keep the economy in equilibrium by taking new wives when there is a glut of them on the market, or conversely, to sell the children of her wives for cattle when there are too many cattle and not enough wives in any village. By native terminology, the queen is the "father" of any child born to a member of her harem. In actuality, only the "cabinet" and visiting royalty from other tribes may mate with any of the queen's "wives."

When we finally arrived at the queen's house, a large square "European" (the local euphemism for white) type of house, we were led along a wide verandah, at the corner of which we encountered a group of barefoot men on the floor. Rounding the corner, we saw more men seated on either side of the verandah, and at the far end of it, three women, two elderly and one very young. Here at last was the object of our visit—the wonderful, omnipotent, eternal, legendary She. For all that she in no way resembled Rider Haggard's ravishing heroine, she had an innate dignity of bearing and was obviously a queen, albeit a semi-savage one. She was seated on a leopard skin, and due to the inclement weather had a cheap woolen blanket thrown about her shoulders, otherwise she was naked to the waist. Her skirt was flimsy blue polka-dot "missionary cloth". About her ankles and wrists she wore a large number of brass and iron rings, the same as those worn by practically all native women in South Africa. The only outward sign of her royalty was her shaved head. Only members of the royal family were allowed to shave their heads completely.

As a special prerogative, we were allowed to retain our shoes and also walk or stand in the queen's presence. Native protocol calls for the removal of shoes by those modern (and rich) enough to own them, and also demands that all persons crawl on hands and knees whenever in the royal presence. We were immediately presented to the queen, who greeted us with the traditional native type of handclasp, consisting of each party grasping the right thumb of the other. After the introductions Lombard made the formal speech indulged in by natives all over Africa, during which each party tries to outdo the other with compliments and expressions of pleasure at seeing the other, at being able to offer hospitality, at being able to visit the justly famed home, etc. This over, we got to the next part of the ceremony, that of presenting our gift to the queen. The traditional gift is a goat, but since it was crowded enough in the Ford sedan with us and our luggage, we had no desire for the added company of a goat. Instead we presented the queen with the price of a goat and expressed our hope that it would not inconvenience her to purchase one. To make up for our slight breach of etiquette we also brought a kerchief of brightly printed chiffon, which seemed to interest the queen not at all, but which evidently attracted the queen's lady-in-waiting (also her sister) very much. The third woman, the young girl, with a partially shaved head, turned out to be one of the queen's wives, and was at this party in the role of Hebe. It was she who dispensed the beer contained in a large earthenware pot.

Having now completed the diplomatic protocol, we were invited to sit with the rest of the guests (who were the "cabinet" and the "supreme court") and join in the drinking. After we each had a drink the pot was soon emptied, so the other guests and the queen and her attendants departed, leaving us greatly exhilarated by our success so far.

Shortly thereafter, we were taken to a round, windowless kraal belonging to the queen, which had been allotted us. For this we were thankful, for the rain had continued all day, and sleeping outside would have been uncomfortable. We prepared our own supper, partly to relieve Donald's embarrassment at not having anything prepared and also partly to allay our own fears about the sanitary standards of native food.

When we had completed supper and arranged our bedding, we were prepared to sleep, for it had been a strenuous day, but apparently the queen was in a festive mood. She had not had many visitors, and felt duty-bound as a hostess to give a party where we could share the entire pot of beer instead of merely tasting the dregs. We were requested to come immediately to a small kraal beside the Queen's main house. When we arrived, the queen had already established herself on her leopard skin, with her sister beside her. For our especial benefit, six small chairs had been procured, and we were placed in a row just to the right of the entrance, opposite Modjadji herself. We entered and sat down as Donald had told us to do. He then entered on his hands and knees and prostrated himself, with his face avert-

Modjadji

ed from the queen until she gave him permission to take his position to our right. The head man of the tribe entered in similar fashion, as did her beer-pot maiden, as we afterward called her. Her job was no simple one, for she had the task of not only prostrating herself and crawling across the floor, but also of managing the very large and obviously heavy pot of beer at the same time.

A small kerosene lamp was lighted and the formal ceremony began. Everyone waited until the queen gave the signal to her sister to start the serving of the beer. The sister thereupon took the queen's special handleless gourd and passed it to the servant, instructing her to fill it. The girl did so, using another gourd as a dipper. She then drank from the bowl before returning it, performing, no doubt, the time-honored ritual of the king's taster. Whenever the queen drank, all present made obeisance. Aside from the queen's, there was only one drinking gourd, no matter how many guests. This was filled and given to the queen's sister, who retained it until she had emptied it, after which it was returned to the pot for refilling. It was then given to the head man, who did likewise. Next it was passed to Donald, then to Mr. Mothivi, and finally to us. To our regret, we found that the gourd held almost a pint. The taste of Kaffir beer is abominable, and its strength is immediately apparent. There were no potted plants in which to pour it, and lingering over it was considered bad form, as you would then be holding up the other guests. So there was nothing to do but gulp it down as rapidly as possible. We thus kept on drinking and chatting with the queen through Donald and her sister. Although we were sitting not more than six feet from her, she always maintained the fiction that she heard nothing, and would always wait until Donald had translated to the sister who in turn then repeated everything to the queen. She would even wait poker-faced for jokes to be repeated officially. Once the story had thus reached her she would react appropriately. At this point the queen inquired where each of us lived, a matter of importance among Africans in identifying your tribal loyalties. America was a vague concept for the natives, but when it was explained that I had come all the way across the great water to pay homage to the queen, an audible murmur ran through the group, and for the remainder of the visit I was noticeably an object of curiosity.

After a while we were called on to sing for the queen. Our raucous, somewhat bawdy, student songs apparently pleased her, for she informed us that she considered us her own children, adopting us forthwith into the tribe. Since she is the mother of the sun, we decided that made us stepbrothers! Soon thereafter the supply of beer was exhausted and we were allowed to depart, semi-divine by royal fiat, and completely drunk by natural process.

After breakfast the next morning, we said that we had to be on our way and would like to express our thanks to the queen for her hospitality. Donald sent off a message immediately, and within about fifteen minutes we were on the verandah again, confronting another pot of beer, which by this time we believed to be as eternal as Modjadji herself. We finally got around to requesting permission to take photos, and were pleasantly surprised when the queen agreed. After we had taken all the photos, drunk all the beer and paid the ritual compliments, we rose to go, and paid what we intended to be our final and all-inclusive compliment. Lombard said—in the queen's native language, so that there would be no question of editing in Donald's translation—that we had enjoyed out visit, etcetera, and that the only thing that could have made it better would have been some sunshine to insure our photos. It seems that we should simply have departed, for we spoiled an otherwise perfect record in observing the intricate native protocol. Donald immediately interrupted to inform us that on the contrary, we should consider ourselves fortunate. It was not every group of visitors to whom the queen was inclined to demonstrate her powers, and in fact, the rain had been caused in our especial honor. And indeed, just as our car reached the bottom of the hill and the village disappeared from sight, the sun came out from behind the clouds.

While flying back to New York, I began thinking about "She" and the experience related above. By the time I landed in New York, I had decided to break into fresh ground and immediately telephoned back to Florida and ordered the Haggard collection. To my delight, it sold out lock, stock and barrel as soon as I catalogued the collection. And it spurred me to carry more nineteenth-century material whenever I could obtain it.

Barbara Howes

My friendship with Barbara Howes evolved slowly. The first contact was by mail, as with virtually all of my early friendships with poets. She and her then husband William Jay Smith were two of the younger poets whose works had been recommended to me by my friend George Firmage, the bibliographer of e.e. cummings. When I had acquired all of their works, I wrote for permission to send the accumulated volumes to them for autographing, permission which they generously granted at once. Not too long after that I began my tenure at the Phoenix. One evening a large-boned lady came into the shop accompanied by her teen-age son. This was Barbara Howes, bringing me a batch of her manuscript work sheets to be appraised as a donation to the American Literature Collection in the Beinecke Library at Yale. Dr. Donald Gallup was then in charge of the American Literature part of the Beinecke, and had recommended me to her.

This was in the days before Congress decided that the self-generated papers (their pedestrian term for poets' manuscripts) were no longer tax deductible as institutional gifts. Ms. Howes, like several other poets, was donating manuscripts to major university libraries on a yearly basis. I was happy to meet the poet personally, and quickly made the required appraisal. This procedure was repeated every year until Congress lowered the boom. Around that time her marriage was dissolved and she continued to reside in the large old farmhouse that she and her husband had occupied in North Pownal, a remote hamlet in Vermont about ten miles south of Bennington..

Our meetings had always been pleasant, and I continued to send her each new book for inscribing. At some point, Barbara asked me and my housemate, Kenneth Doubrava, to come for a visit. We accepted immediately, and set out by car. After a couple of false turns, we eventually reached the large yellow frame house. We were greeted by a small pack of noisy but not aggressive dogs; Barbara herself emerged to greet us, and in we went. After we had freshened up, we went downstairs to meet the rest of the household, which consisted of a small pug dog named Ivan, along with a previously encountered Great Dane, Echo, and an assortment of cats.

There was a library—large and well-filled with books I was eager to examine—which contained surplus furniture, stacks of magazines, and mysterious unmarked bundles. Obviously it was not a room in daily use. Social life centered around the living room with a large fireplace, the dining room, and the kitchen. While the house sat directly on the narrow country road, it was actually perched on a narrow strip of flat land, for immediately behind the house the land dropped precipitously some fifty feet or more down to a tiny creek, beside which a swimming pool and a sauna had been installed. Over the years we used the pool often, but the sauna only once when her son Greg was at home and could fire it up.

As part of our hostess gift, we had brought some excellent steaks from New York. Alas, we very quickly learned that whatever other accomplishments were in Barbara's repertoire, cooking was not one of them, for the steaks were burned almost to a crisp.

The next morning everyone drifted down on his own schedule, and made his own breakfast accompanied by the resident menagerie. Later that day, as we lounged around the pool, Barbara asked what we would like for dinner that night. Kenneth, an excellent cook, volunteered then and there to take over for the remaining meals. Barbara readily acquiesced, and this established a pattern that remained in place throughout the many succeeding visits.

So with a shopping list in hand, Barbara offered to drive us in to Bennington to procure the various items which Kenneth needed. It was very hot August day, and we had not finished our drinks. Barbara had just begun a can of beer.

"Come on," she said, "We'll finish these on the way." Kenneth and I shot questioning glances at each other, but we both shrugged our shoulders, deciding that since we were in the country, Barbara certainly must have felt that there was no likelihood of being stopped by the police. Just how unlikely this proved to be, we very soon found out.

So we piled into the Saab, and off we went. We were scarcely on the road when Barbara informed us that there was a long detour caused by road repair work, but she knew a shortcut we could take. With that we left the dirt road and started across a field, going up a steep hill. It was rough going, requiring both hands on the wheel. Barbara accomplished this by wedging the beer can between her knees. Obviously she was a lady with an extremely practical, no-nonsense approach to life's little problems.

Our visit was, apparently, a great success all around, for this was the beginning of a great many reciprocal visits until we sold the New York town house and moved to Maryland. We would go up to Vermont for a weekend in the summer, and Barbara would stay with us during her winter visits to New York for a poetry reading or for personal shopping. Between these visits she would quite often send me drafts of new poems for criticism. On our visits to Pownal, as often as not, one of the cats would decide to sleep with one or the other of us in the guest room

The first time I mentioned this to Barbara she started laughing and told us about the time that Eudora Welty was a guest, and after everyone had gone to bed, she and Bill were startled to hear Eudora crying out, "No, Bill, no! Go away!." Since Bill was in bed, he and Barbara couldn't figure out what was going on. They got up, and found it was one of the cats scratching at the guest room door that had caused Miss Welty to think that something more suspicious was happening.

Because of their proximity to Bennington,, Barbara and Bill had quite often played hosts to visiting literati, as the signatures in their guest book will attest—Richard Wilbur, Robert Frost, Dylan Thomas, W.H. Auden, Theodore Roethke, Isak Dinesen, to name only some of the brightest stars in the literary constellation. Sometimes Bill and Barbara provided more than just a place to stay. Barbara claimed with pride that it was she who taught W.H. Auden how to drive.

One weekend was the scene of a rather harrowing experience. It had grown quite late, and I finally decided to go to bed. But Barbara was in a confiding mood, and wanted to talk to Kenneth. He somehow elicits confidences, especially from the female sex. I must say that he has always kept these matters totally secret, even from me. Suddenly I was awakened by a very alarmed Kenneth, who burst into the bedroom crying, "Barbara fell over the banister and I think she's dead!"

I immediately jumped out of bed and came to the railing. There was Barbara lying supine on the floor below. It certainly looked ominous. What had happened was that when they had finished talking, Barbara had preceded Kenneth up the stairs, carrying some books. He was behind her carrying the pug, Ivan, whose hind legs were so weak that he could not climb the stairs, which were a rather long flight due to the height of the ground floor, some thirteen feet or so. Barbara had caught her heel in the carpeting and had catapulted over the railing. Kenneth had been unable to catch her, and there she lay.

We immediately dialed 911, but then couldn't tell them where we were. There were lots of old farmhouses on narrow country roads, and as often as we had visited, we had never actually known the name of the road. So we told them we'd call back as soon as we could phone her son Greg in New York and get the information. We certainly gave poor Greg a fright awakening him at 2 a.m. with this alarming news. He told me the name of the road, the Mount Anthony Road, and we called the police back with the location. The ambulance arrived promptly.

By this time Barbara had come to, but we insisted that she lie still, for who could know what bones she might have broken. When the medics arrived they examined her and wanted her to go to the hospital for X-rays, as we also thought should be done. But she refused. We insisted, but she was adamant, and the medics said that they were not allowed to take anyone against his will. So we could do nothing more than apologize to them and help Barbara into bed, along with her faithful Ivan.

The next morning she said that she felt sore and bruised but otherwise was all right. We insisted that she stay in bed all the next day. By the time we were ready to leave Sunday afternoon she was up and about, apparently none the worse for wear. We reported back to Greg who said that he would come up from New York that evening, so we felt that it would be all right for us to leave.

A couple of years after we moved to Maryland and no longer were making the annual visits, there was a large party given in honor of her seventy-fifth birthday. Much as we hated to miss it, we were unable to go, for it was to take place at the same time that we were performing in a local production of *Amadeus*. So instead I composed a bit of doggerel to be read at the festivities. Great poetry it certainly wasn't, but it did provide some amusement from the fact that I mentioned every one of her books in it, as follows:

Hail to thee, blithe Barbara
Bard thou never wert.
All hail to the only bard in
Pownal with a *Blue Garden*
Who knows that being an *Undersea Farmer*
Will never harm her.
Who writes for free
In the cold country
In both *Light and Dark*
Next to neighbors called Park,
Who, while *Looking Up at Leaves*
From her room under the eaves
Sends *A Private Signal* to Ivan
With Echo asleep on the divan.
Who, all things proving,
Delights us with *Moving*.
Now all join in wishin' her
Good luck with *The Road Commissioner*
And much luck from two men
Who here sign themselves Bob and Ken.

Michael McClure

My first encounter with the poet Michael McClure occurred in 1966 on my first trip to San Francisco. Getting to his home wasn't easy. He lived then at the top of one of San Francisco's steepest hills, so steep that there were no connecting streets and the taxi took a lot longer than I had expected, circling around until we finally reached the proper street. The result of this was that I arrived forty-five minutes late. The McClures were also upset, understandably, since they too had been a few minutes late in arriving home and were afraid that I had arrived earlier and gone away when I found no one at home.

The anxiety soon passed as the McClures led me to the top of the two-storied frame house, apparently built just after the earthquake of 1912. The view from the bedroom and the living room windows was one of the most superb in San Francisco, looking out over the entire city, the bay, the bridge and the surrounding area. These two rooms were divided only by a very wide archway, just barely indicating a division. Two double beds had been joined against the wall of the bedroom so they faced a working fireplace in the living room. There were two chairs and a table with a portable type-writer on it in the living room, and bookshelves (with a surprisingly small number of books) flanking the fireplace.

The dominating feature of the room was an enormous original poster of Jean Harlow in *Hell's Angels* hanging on a side wall. The remaining decorations were paintings by Bruce Connor. Over the bed hung both the large and small versions of McClure's *Love Lion Lioness* poster with portraits of Jean Harlow and Billy the Kid.

Robert Duncan and Michael McClure, San Francisco

Michael was a bit shorter than I had expected, being approximately five feet nine inches tall, with a delicately boned, very refined face. His eyes seemed small and searching. He had let his hair grow long at that period; it did not present the "Jesus" appearance of so many of the Beatniks, but instead gave an immediate and startling leonine appearance, especially when he threw his head back to laugh, which he did frequently. He was wearing boots (with the trouser legs on the outside, black, tight-fitting chinos) and a black waist-length leather jacket.

Joanna, his then wife, was an extremely good-looking woman, poised, with flair and natural grace. She was wearing bell-bottom white slacks, a black jersey sweater, and a single strand of pearls. She looked elegant enough to be ready to pose then and there for fashion photos. After the introductions, she left us to attend to the needs of their daughter, the McClure's only child.

While she was out of the room, Michael picked up his new Autoharp and took a pose, holding it high on his left shoulder. I was immediately struck by the image of a modern Orpheus with his lute. He shook the hair out of his eyes and started to sing. He moved about just enough to call it dancing, giving a sort of triple performance—playing the harp, singing, and dancing, evolving a natural and interesting style all his own. He sang several of his own *Ghost Tantras* as well as the text that appeared on the *Love Lion Lioness* poster.

Then Joanna returned and suggested that we all go out to eat, as it was then eight o'clock. This caused a great deal of commotion, since there were four of us, counting their lovely, very blonde daughter (who was then nine years old) and much discussion about the cars. The McClure's family car could hold all four of us but couldn't make it up the hills with all of us in it. So it was finally decided that Joanna and their daughter would go in the family car, and Michael would take me in his newly acquired sports car, a red British Triumph.

We arrived in Chinatown some twenty minutes ahead of the distaff side of the family, thanks primarily to Michael's "hot-rod" style of driving, a precarious thing in San Francisco, perhaps more so than in most other major cities. The restaurant was one of the most elegant in Chinatown, and Michael's appearance caused a great deal of staring by the startled, conservatively dressed patrons. When the McClure ladies arrive there ensued yet another comic scene. The waiter brought us three menus which when opened showed one page entirely in Chinese, underneath which was a listing in English. But somehow Michael was convinced that there were delicacies on the Chinese list which did not appear in the English list, and kept insisting that the Chinese list be translated for us. As in many Chinese restaurants, the waiter spoke very little English, and kept turning the page back to the English list, insisting that everything appeared there. For a while I despaired of ever getting anything to eat, all the while being reminded of Buddy Hackett's Chinese waiter routine from the Ed Sullivan show in the early days of television.

Finally some sort of compromise was apparently reached, for there soon began a procession of dishes which could have fed twice the number of people in our party. The feast included bird's nest soup, some sort of fish, lobster in black bean salt, an enormous plate of curried crabs, and squab, which surprised us greatly since the waiter had pronounced it in such a manner that we expected squid.

When we left we again split into two parties. It then developed that Michael couldn't remember where he had parked the car. I hadn't tried at all to commit it to memory, so for the next twenty minutes or so we ran all over Chinatown looking in back alleys and narrow streets for the car, with me thinking we would be mugged, if not worse, at any minute. No sooner had we found the car and started on our way, than Michael began complaining how hungry he was, rather surprising after the huge dinner we had all eaten. Finally he drew up abruptly at a corner drug store, went in, and bought twenty candy bars, several of which he consumed on the remainder of the trip back to his home.

When we got there, Michael's wife and daughter had apparently gone to bed. He showed me an enormous trunkful of manuscripts of unpublished plays and poems. I asked him twice during the evening about the possibility of the Phoenix publishing something by him, but both times he said that he was finished with books, except for wanting to see *Dark Brown* back in print. He was convinced at that time that rock and roll music was the wave of the future and that books were rapidly becoming a thing of the past. This disheartening observation rather crippled the conversation, for me at least.

Photo by Ken Howard

Michael McClure

To cheer me up, Michael took up his Autoharp again and sang some more of the *Ghost Tantras* for me, dancing as before. I wondered what the neighbors below us thought of this, since it was now past midnight. When he paused momentarily I asked him. He laughed, replying "I don't know; I suppose they enjoy it since they have never complained."

I asked him then if he had ever performed for an audience, and he said, "Well no, not really, unless you count the lions in the San Francisco Zoo."

"What do you mean?"

"When I first got the idea of beast language poems, I got friendly with the lion-keeper out at the zoo, and got him to let me stay in the lion house after the zoo had closed for the day, so that only he and I were in the lion house with the lions. I sang several of the *Ghost Tantras,* but nothing happened. We were both disappointed, and he wanted to give up, but I decided to try one more time, and towards the end of it the lioness began to roar back, and then all the others joined in."

"Really?"

"No kidding. So a couple of days later I came back with a tape machine and recorded it—and the same thing happened!"

I smiled and said I'd like to hear the tape.

"My tape machine is broken, but I'll give you a tape."

And sure enough, when I got back to New York and played it for Lorelei, my very ancient Siamese cat, she at first ignored it, but upon a second playing, roused herself and "sang" back, just as Michael said the lioness in the zoo had done.

Luckily for poetry and drama and for all us book-lovers, Michael's gloomy prediction has not come true. And even better for everyone he has gone on producing books and plays for our enjoyment. While never a "household name" the way Frost or Moore or Sandburg were, he has steadfastly maintained his brilliance and innovative daring, and more often than not, scoring a hit. Especially in his plays he keeps pushing the boundaries.

This initial acquaintance evolved into a close friendship so that not long after, Michael regularly stayed *chez moi* on his periodic visits to New York. One of these was in 1979 to attend the Obie awards for the best Off-Broadway performances of the preceding year. Michael received the Best Play award for his *Josephine the Mouse-Singer.*

The event was of course televised. It so happened that the succeeding day coincided with our cleaning woman's biweekly visit. She became very excited when she saw Michael in the house. Here, before her eyes, was a bona fide celebrity. She had encountered many notable people in the arts at my house: poets, novelists, painters, dancers. But Michael she had seen on television! She immediately requested him to write something for her, so, gracious as always, he wrote out a short poem for her. I'm sure that Clara wanted something to back up her claim among her circle of friends that she actually met a television celebrity.

Eve Merriam

One of the most enchanting persons I encountered in all the years of involvement in the literary world was Eve Merriam. Not as widely acclaimed as she should have been, she most nearly fits the eighteenth-century appellation "Man of Letters." Her talents were wide-ranging. Starting as a poet, she went on to create a long series of highly successful children's books; several volumes of superb, witty, acerbic poetry; biographies; social criticism; short fiction; television scripts; and an enormously successful long-running Off-Broadway musical.

I first met Eve in the early summer of 1950 as a result of my writing to her to ask her to sign my copies of some of her books—a practice that was to result in several important literary friendships. In the years just prior to this I had started to read several new young poets through the guidance a friend, George Firmage. He recommended that I try, among others, Eve Merriam, one of a group whose careers were just then getting started. Actually, Eve's career was already flourishing. It had gotten started with an initial boost when her first book *Family Circle* was published in the distinguished Yale Younger Poets series. She told me she had tried several times to break into the series, and had submitted a totally different group of poems each time, not realizing that this was not necessary. The age limit for a "younger poet" was thirty, so at age twenty-nine she decided to give it one last try and was actually assembling yet another group of poems when word arrived that one of her previous submissions had been accepted.

After this she was published in 1944 by New Directions in their short-lived series (of three volumes) entitled Five Young American Poets, which consisted of full-length books of poems by five young writers. When I handed her my copy at our first meeting in her apartment on Central Park West at Sixty-eighth Street, she was surprised to see that I had located one, informing me that the edition was small due to wartime paper restrictions, and that it was already bringing premium prices.

She then started laughing, saying "I want to tell you a story about this book. It's like one of those stories that has as its punch line 'and that woman was Eleanor Roosevelt." Well, before this book came out I was talking to Audrey Wood and she said, 'I've got this crackpot young writer whose plays haven't been produced, but they will be. He writes poetry too. Where can I get him published?' I suggested New directions where I had some early pieces published in their annuals. And of course, that crackpot young writer was Tennessee Williams."

In any event, he was published in the final volume, along with Eve herself, John Frederick Nims, Jean Garrigue, and a South American poet named Alejandro Carrion who has never been heard from since. She then got back to signing the rest of the books I had brought. When she came to the last one she said, "Let's be dashing about this," and boldly drew a line through her printed name, signing below, saying, "Auden did that for me once, and I've never gotten over it." Years later, when I first met Auden after a similar request to have some books signed, I noticed that he habitually did just as she had told me.

At that time I was working with George Firmage on a projected comprehensive volume of bibliographies of current American poets (which, alas, never came to fruition when Firmage's interest flagged in favor of a bibliography of e.e. cummings.) I discussed this project with Eve, asking her if she had published any private pamphlets. It turned out that indeed there had been one, a memoir of her mother, a copy of which she immediately gave to me.

She suggested that a good place to do further research was the poetry collection at the University of Buffalo, at that time one of the very few American institutions collecting current materials in the field of poetry. I told her that I knew of their interest in this field through their publication of *Four Poets on Poetry* which included inter alia Karl Shapiro, a fellow Baltimorean and my first poetic enthusiasm. She asked if I knew him, adding that they were longtime close friends, having gotten their starts together, he having been published in an earlier *Five Young American Poets*. Their friendship did not, however, affect her critical judgment, saying that his earlier poetry was much better than what he was currently producing, adding, "His criticism is sheer nonsense. His article on T.S. Eliot is clownish and impossible. Mind you, it's perfectly all right not to like Eliot, but you cannot escape the fact that neither you nor I nor anyone else writing today would be writing if it were not for Eliot. He's simply crazy to say that 'all political poetry is third-rate.' Why, that would knock down everybody from Homer to Milton, and on down." I asked her how she felt about Pound on that score. "Well," she replied, "I was asked to sign a petition against his being awarded the Bollingen Prize, but I refused because I had not read the poems at that time." She went on to say that after she had read them she thought that while some of *The Cantos* were obscure, his tirades against the Italians and the Jews were crystal clear. "I still don't think that he should not be published. Publish everything and let the future decide. But don't give him awards."

I then asked her about Gertrude Stein; she replied that she had not read anything, but wanted to read *Three Lives* soon. I suggested that she also try *Things As They Are.* This was Stein's first piece of fiction but not published until after her death because of its Lesbian theme. Her diction is straightforward and completely clear, refuting totally the frequent charge that she did not know how to write grammatically correct English.

Next I asked Eve if any of her poems had been set to music, since Ned Rorem was at that time working assiduously in creating musical settings for poems by a wide variety of younger poets.

"I don't think you'll find anything of mine published that way," replied Eve, "I attract mostly folk-singers. And most of what has been used comes out of *Montgomery, Alabama and Money, Mississippi* and sung by various people in some very strange places. I met Kenneth Rexroth in Paris a couple of years ago, and he said to me, ' I've just come from Prague and went to a nightclub there that had been recommended to me as a hangout for the wild young set. You'll never guess what the entertainment was.' "Well, what?" I asked.

"'Your poems from *Montgomery,* read in Czech to music by Duke Ellington.'"

"So you see what I mean by very strange places!"

As I rose to go she had a further comment about Karl Shapiro, saying that such wild statements as he had made recently could only be made by someone who was "terribly young and therefore an *enfant terrible,* or some grand old man like Robert Graves, who could get away with anything." And Karl was neither.

Over the succeeding years until her death in 1992 we remained very good, close friends. She was often at our house, always at our Christmas parties, and frequently a guest at dinner. At one of these she made such an impression on Bill Cagle, then in charge of the Lilly Library at Indiana University in Bloomington, that he added her at once to the roster of American poets being collected by them, and also sought to purchase her manuscript archive. And we were also frequent guests at her apartment. One such party was unquestionably unique; she hosted a publication party for a book by a friend of hers dealing with the history of chocolate. Every major chocolate manufacturer in the United States and Europe set up enormous displays of their wares, from which we guests were free to sample as much as we wanted, along with a fine vintage champagne. Naturally no one could eat very much of such a surfeit of sweet, but we were all provided with capacious "doggie bags". I still wonder, though, whatever became of the enormous Hershey Bar that was so large it completely covered Eve's grand piano.

Always gracious, Eve, on learning that I had sold my town house, was unable to find a place to stay, and was living rather uncomfortably in the back of my shop, turned her apartment over to me while she was away on tour. She was one of two poet friends who responded in this manner, Allen Ginsberg being the other.

Although primarily known as a poet, her theater work was extensive and included *We the Women,* a television program that was in fact the first network documentary on women's rights. Her musical *The Club* was directed by Tommy Tune at the beginning of his career. It was a trenchant statement about sexism, in which members of a turn-of-the-century men's club indulged in sexist remarks and attitudes. Making the point all the sharper was the fact that the cast was totally female in men's garb. This garnered an Obie, and had an extremely long run in New York as well as productions world-wide.

For me her wit was the keenest of anyone's I've ever encountered. At the end of her book *Fig Leaf,* a devastating study of the women's fashion business, she appended a stiletto-sharp glossary deflating the chichés and hyperbole endemic to the trade. For example "exclusive" she defines as "a product offered to the widest possible market." "Timeless" means "a style that remains in fashion for more than one season." Her deftness was so unerring that it discomfited a great many people who became her targets. Her book of poems *The Inner City Mother Goose,* which drew heavily on sharp paraphrases of well known Mother Goose rhymes applied to the problems of inner city life, was attacked by judges, police chiefs and others, who claimed that she was glamorizing crime and lawlessness. At the same time that her play *Out of Our Father's House* was being broadcast on Public Television's "Great Performances" series she was attacked in congress, where a bill was proposed (but never passed) to have her work banned in schools and libraries throughout the nation. This did not deter President Carter from inviting her to read at The White House.

Eve was probably most succinctly summed up by a friend of mine, who, after I cajoled him into reading *Fig Leaf,* declared, "My God, that woman's a female Mencken."

Marianne Serves Lunch

arianne Moore was the first poet whom I got to know really well. It all came about as the result of my writing her a fan letter asking if she would by willing to sign my copies of some of her books. This was in 1959, well before I had any ideas of owning a book shop. I had only recently come back to my true love, poetry, and its pendant, collecting first editions of a few authors whose work I admired. I had at first been advised by the dealers whose shops I frequented not to try to collect Moore in any serious fashion due to the generally accepted fact that her second book, a small pamphlet entitled *Marriage,* was so scarce as never to be seen, and generally categorized as hopeless.

Almost equally daunting was the problem of her first book entitled simply *Poems.* It was issued privately in 1921 without her knowledge by a group of friends headed by the British author Winifred Ellerman, who preferred to be known by her pseudonym, Bryher. I did know where one of these was to be found, but I accepted the received wisdom about *Marriage* (which had also been published by a friend, this time Monroe Wheeler) and did not purchase *Poems.* So I did not seriously consider forming a Moore collection, despite my intense admiration for her work. That is, until one fortuitous day in 1960 while accompanying my parents on a trip to Europe.

At that time I had just started collecting Gertrude Stein, and while in London I went to the prestigious firm of Bertram Rota, Ltd, looking for elusive Stein titles. I was greeted by a young man at the front desk who was very cordial, especially after I revealed that my quest was for Stein. He turned out to be Arthur Uphill, then as now an ardent Steinophile. But while we were discussing my needs in the Stein canon, my eye lit on a small blue pamphlet on his desk. Unbelievably, there lay a copy of the "impossible" *Marriage*—the very thing that kept everyone from forming complete Moore collections. Trying to conceal my elation, I asked the price and was astonished at being told that it was a mere two pounds. Naturally I bought it at once, figuring that if I had the supposedly impossible title, the rest would be easy. This was not the case, as I was subsequently to learn. At least two other titles proved far more difficult to locate.

As soon as I returned to the United States, I went to the University Place Bookshop, then still under the ownership of its founder, Walter Goldwater. It was there that I had seen a copy of her first book, the 1921 *Poems*. Alas, it had been sold, but Walter was kind enough to tell me to whom he had sold it, Julia Newman, another dealer. I immediately went to her shop, and although I was a bit unhappy that the price had increased from $12.50 to $20.00, I bought it, thank goodness! That price was, in fact a very reasonable markup, and of course by today's prices a laughably low price.

Now owning the two difficult first titles, as well as several subsequent books, I wrote asking permission to take them to Miss Moore for signing. She, as was her custom, replied promptly and graciously, suggesting that I mail the books to her, but that if I feared for their safety in the mails (which I did) I might bring them to her apartment in Brooklyn some evening after she returned from a short anticipated journey. With perhaps more zeal than regard for her time, I opted at once for the visit. A date was set and off I went, straight from work at the cuckoo clock factory, armed with a bouquet of yellow flowers, a bit of serendipity as yellow turned out to be her favorite color, at least in flowers.

The Brooklyn apartment was the usual old-fashioned railroad flat. A long corridor ran along the left wall, with a bedroom and a bathroom on the right, and then opened into a cluster of three rooms at the end of the corridor, consisting of a living room, dining room and kitchen. But the dining room was not functioning as such, since it still contained a large brass double bed which had been her mother's, despite the fact that Mrs. Moore had died several years earlier.

We sat in the living room, which was also her study or work room, and while she was signing the books, my gaze wandered about, noting various pictures, bric-a-brac and the furnishings, until my eye was arrested at the doorway leading from the living room into the hallway. At the top of the

Marianne Moore in The Phoenix

door frame was what looked for all the world like a trapeze bar, hanging very high up, suspended by two chains. I looked and looked, but could come to no other conclusion but that it must be a trapeze. But at her age? (She was then in her seventies, and rather frail).

My curiosity finally got the better of my manners, and I asked, "Miss Moore, what is that hanging up there in the doorway?"

Without looking up from the inscribing she replied, "Oh, that's my trapeze," and then added, as though as an afterthought, "I don't use it much anymore."

When she had finished signing and correcting all the books I had brought, she got up and went to a closet and brought out a copy of her latest book which was to be published a few days hence—*O To Be a Dragon*. While inscribing it she related what a fight she had had with the publisher, who tastelessly at first used pseudo-Chinese lettering on the title page simply because of the word "dragon." It was my first realization that authors seldom have any control over the physical appearance of their books.

At that time I had no idea that there would be any further visits. It seemed that I had made a favorable impression, for a sporadic correspondence developed, usually about my bringing or sending the latest additions to my collection for inscribing. Sometimes more sprightly matters were discussed, such as in the charming sequence of letters involving the selection of a new cuckoo clock to replace the one I had noticed no longer in working order in her long hallway.

I had offered either to have the old one repaired at my work place, or to replace it with a new one. As matters turned out, some other friends with the same idea sent her a new one while she was making her decision about style. So as a token I sent her a miniature version in commemoration of our conversation. It was still in her possession at the time of her death many years later, and is, I believe, still to be seen in her living room, now installed in its entirety at the Rosenbach Museum in Philadelphia.

Her hair was by then totally white, with no trace of the red for which she had been famous in the poetic circles of her younger days. She had apparently never cut it, for a long braid wound about the back and the top of her head, held in place by long, old-fashioned tortoise-shell hairpins, to make a small bun which doubtless served as the anchor for her famous tricorn hat.

The Brooklyn neighborhood where she had lived for so many years, first with her mother and then alone, had once been an upper-class area, but over the years had declined so steadily as to be alarming to her brother and to many of her friends. She resided on the top floor, the sixth I recall, of a once elegant apartment building, now sadly run-down.

I was quietly amused one day when paying a daytime visit to witness a small vignette as I stepped from the elevator. Miss Moore was standing in her doorway to receive me. Just at that point the adjacent door opened and out stepped a blowzy woman, an archetypal prostitute, complete with the obligatory cigarette drooping from her lower lip as she inquired of Miss Moore, "I'm going out. Can I get you anything, honey?"

Apparently even the neighborhood hookers felt protective towards her. On another occasion, when I was leaving, she wanted to go out and do some shopping for herself, and accompanied me to the subway station. This time I was treated to her legendary powers of observation and also to her felicitous phrase-making. Ahead of us three plump young girls, clad in slacks far too tight, were sauntering along. Almost under her breath Miss Moore remarked, "Three graces ungracious."

Somewhat against her own wishes she finally gave in to the pressures of her brother and various friends, and agreed to move back to Manhattan, to a safe, modern building on West Ninth Street in Greenwich Village, just west of Fifth Avenue, not far from her original residence before world War I. In preparation for the move she had tried to reduce the bulk of her library somewhat, and had divided what she wanted to dispose of into three more or less equal lots. These were to be sold to three book-dealer friends: Frances Steloff of the Gotham Book Mart, her intimate friend for many decades; Margie Cohn of the House of Books, who had published Moore's only play *The Absentee* in a deluxe, limited edition; and myself, who by that time had acquired the Phoenix Book Shop.

I was both pleased and flattered that she regarded me highly enough to be included in her largesse. Trying to be as equable as possible, she had divided everything into several shopping bags for each of us. I don't know exactly what the two ladies received, but in my share were some ordinary books, probably review copies; several magazines with annotations at her contributions; and a large number of real treasures. Included in my lot were several titles inscribed to her by T.S. Eliot, including the four original separate pamphlets comprising the *Four Quartets,* as well as his pamphlet *The Three Voices of Poetry* inscribed to her "humbly, T.S. Eliot". One acquaintance of mine opined that it was probably the only time he ever used that word. Moore had penciled in several comments, including one remark "this passage won't do."

Also present were rare early limited editions of William Carlos Williams, the privately printed novels of H.D. and a myriad assortment of other treasures. I had brought them back to the shop and had just gone through them rather quickly in order to send payment to Miss Moore, when in walked in Clive Driver, then director of the Rosenbach Museum. He asked what was in the shopping bags spread around my desk, and on being told what was in them, asked permission to go through the lot. After he had done so he startled me by asking to buy the lot *in toto*. I wasn't prepared for this, having planned to make these rarities the featured items in my next catalog. He explained that he also wanted to try to purchase the portions that had gone to Miss Steloff and to Mrs. Cohn. He then surprised me by asking if I thought Miss Moore would be amenable to talking to him about the possible eventual purchase of her entire archive.

Reluctantly, I sold him the entire lot and agreed to broach the idea to her the next time I visited her. I suggested this approach due to the fact that a small stroke had impaired her speech slightly, and although talking with her vis-à-vis presented no problem, telephone conversations could be somewhat difficult. Shortly thereafter a new book of hers was published, giving me the opportunity to visit her to have it signed. As promised, I suggested the possibility of the transfer of her entire archive to the Rosenbach Foundation, as it by then was named.

There then ensued several years of patient, low-keyed, intermittent discussions regarding the ultimate disposal of her papers. The Rosenbach wasn't the only institution interested—so was the University of Texas at Austin, at that time spending prodigious sums for the purchase of manuscripts and entire archives. Conceivably, Texas could offer more money, so the proper approach, I felt, was to emphasize her longtime personal association with Philadelphia (she was a Bryn Mawr graduate), and the fact that her papers would be accessible to her and to scholars far more readily than if they were all the way off in Texas.

For all her seeming fragility, she was as well armored as her admired pangolin, and one who not easily forgot her Irish ancestry. She could, if provoked, be quite deft at the parry. Once, I was vouchsafed a rare glimpse of her strength when she told me about an incident concerning an article about her friend, the sculptor Malvina Hoffman, which she had originally intended to sell to the *New York Times*. Just at that time Texas renewed its wooing of her and one of their methods of persuasion was to ask her for something to be printed in *The Texas Quarterly*. In the not unreasonable belief that payment would be as generous as their offer for her archive, she sent them the article. When she related this to me she was obviously angered—it was the only time in our long association that I ever heard her raise her voice—Texas had sent her a mere one hundred dollars for the article. She then asked me if I thought that the director of the Rosenbach could come to see her someday soon. I assured her that he would be happy to do so, and as soon as we concluded our conversation I rang up Clive Driver in Philadelphia and conveyed the request. He was ecstatic. This was the opening we had hoped for and had waited for over a period of nearly three years. He came to New York the very next day—October 29, 1968—and over we went with no small amount of trepidation. We had learned that Texas had renewed its campaign recently and had been making increased offers, but was apparently still unaware of the magazine *faux pas*.

With Marianne Moore on her 80th birthday

When we arrived at the apartment we met Louise Crane, Moore's longtime confidante and supporter, and Moore's brother Warner. After the introductions, Moore took Driver on a brief tour of the apartment, pointing out various pictures, objects and keepsakes. We then sat down and chatted for about half an hour, without the subject of the archive being broached at all. In response to a questioning look from Driver I decided that it was probably time for us to depart, both of us feeling rather disappointed.

Perhaps after all she had simply wanted to meet him before coming to a decision. So we rose. But then she said in her breathy *sotto voce* way of speaking, "Do you have to go, Mr. Wilson?"

I assured her that we did not, as we simultaneously sat down immediately. She continued, "You know, Mr. Wilson, that I went down to Texas a couple of weeks ago."

"Yes, Miss Moore, I heard that you had gone."

"Well, they were very nice to me. They flew me down in a special plane, and they showed me the Texas bluebells, which were nice. And they showed me the longhorn cattle, which were also nice. And they took me on a tour of their library, which is very grand indeed. And they said to me, 'Miss Moore, we have here the manuscripts of almost every modern American author, and we'd like to add yours to the collection' I said to them, 'I wouldn't sit down next to most modern American authors.' It won't do, Mr. Wilson, It simply won't do."

And that was how she informed us of her decision in our favor. She looked radiant as she spoke, in better health and spirits than I had seen her for a long time. Driver had previously authorized me to offer her one hundred thousand dollars for her archive, to be paid in installments over a five-year period. This matched the offer from Texas. It was a fair figure at that time, and when I asked if her remarks meant that she agreed to those terms, she replied that she was totally satisfied. Ms. Crane gave an assenting nod. With that Moore rose again and began to enumerate some of the things that would be included in the archive.

First of all, she showed us her famous early working diaries from which she had drawn the inspiration for many of her poems. We handled them very gingerly. With typical modesty she admonished us, "Oh, don't treat them with such reverence. They're not important."

Then she pointed to a tiny bronze elephant by Malvina Hoffman, a painting of roses by e.e. cummings, a watercolor by herself, another by her mother, and then mentioned a series of letters with drawings in them by Gordon Craig, but apologized for not showing them to us, saying, "They're in that drawer over there, but if I open it, I'll not get it shut again."

She also said that there had been a bust of her by Lachaise, given to her by Lincoln Kirstein, but no longer present. "But then he gave it again, this time to a museum."

I asked if she had preserved her correspondence with other poets and authors. With that she opened a file cabinet and pulled out a fat envelope marked "James Joyce" and another surprisingly labeled "Katherine Anne Porter". She showed us her own bound run of *The Dial,* complete, not merely for the years in which she had been its editor. Next she mentioned a box containing the large folio *Cantos* of Ezra Pound "which I can't get down any more," and another, filled with "all those little pamphlets he used to do under all those strange names."

She continued, "I used to have a large bundle of letters from Tom Eliot in that drawer, and when I went to get them copied for Mrs. Eliot I couldn't find them. I ran around like a distracted rat." She did eventually find them, thank goodness!

Her brother Warner started reminiscing about their childhood in St. Louis, and she added an anecdote: "When I was two years old, I pushed a screen open on the second floor and fell out into an oleander bush. My brother picked up the pieces of the bush and brought them into the house to show my mother what had happened to the bush, saying nothing whatever about what had happened to me."

By this time Driver and I had decided that it really was time for us to leave, and as we arose he said that he would have a legal contract drawn up and sent to her very promptly. Escorting us to the door, she said good-bye, adding, "You have saved my life."

Apparently she was as pleased as we were.

....

A little over a year earlier I had been visiting her, but she seemed rather distracted. Sensing that something was bothering her, for she was definitely not her usual self, I rose to go, saying, "Miss Moore, you seem upset or worried about something. Perhaps I should come back another time."

"Oh no," she replied, "It's only that the *New Yorker* just rejected one of my poems. They've never done that before, and I was counting on it to pay the rent this month."

"That's awful," I said, "I can't imagine Howard Moss rejecting a poem of yours."

"It wasn't Howard," she said, not looking up from the book she was signing for me. "He's on vacation. It was his replacement."

She continued inscribing the books, never a simple task for her. She was an inveterate revisionist, and meticulously corrected errors and typos in every book she signed, as well as penning in new versions of well-established poems. While this was in progress, an idea popped into my head. I was appalled at the fact that she might be in desperate financial straits. After her death I learned that she actually had had several thousand dollars, but like many elderly people she felt financially insecure.

"Miss Moore, do you think you could sign a hundred copies if I had the poem printed as a small pamphlet? Because if you could, I'd pay you twice what the *New Yorker* would."

She agreed at once and went into her bedroom, returning with a typescript of *Tipoo's Tiger.* I looked at it to see how long it was, and saw that it would make a superb pamphlet. I asked what her preference was regarding the cover, remembering the discussion of covers, typefaces, and such like at our first meetings. She said that she preferred it to be plain, with no design, and a medium shade of blue. I left almost immediately, striding back to the shop in double triumph—several books inscribed for my personal collection in one hand, and the manuscript for an as yet unpublished Marianne Moore poem in the other.

As soon as I was back in the shop, I started the wheels in motion to have it printed in accordance with her wishes. I got in touch with William Ferguson, a Boston printer whose work I had admired. He readily agreed to do the work, and at a reasonable price. This was fortunate, for I was to discover that I had been a bit rash in offering twice the *New Yorker's* rate—they paid the highest per line rate for poetry of any magazine in America. The work was done impeccably and rather quickly, so that I was able to return during the last week in September, 1967 with one hundred twenty-six copies, one hundred for sale and twenty-six to be lettered for our personal use, thirteen for each of us. Proudly I handed her the forst copy, which she examined meticulously, looking at every page slowly. Then she dumbfounded me by saying, "That last line is all wrong."

"But Miss Moore," I expostulated. "It can't be! I checked the proofs very carefully, and it's exactly the way it reads in the typescript you gave me."

"No, I don't mean it's a printing error. I mean the line itself is simply not right. I'll have to rewrite it."

Dismayed, I said, "But Miss Moore, I can't reprint the entire pamphlet," my heart sinking at the very prospect. Some weeks later it occurred to me that it would not have been a disaster after all—they would have become bibliographical rarities in the form of a suppressed, unissued first state. After considerable discussion between us as to a new working (what nerve I had to make such suggestions!) she decided that she would simply rewrite by hand the last line in all the copies. I was appalled at the idea of so much labor for her, but she was adamant.

The last three lines as originally printed read:
"This ballad still awaits a tiger-hearted bard.
Great losses for the enemy
can not make one's own loss less hard."
Her revised version of the last line read:
"can't make the owner's loss less hard."

At the time, the change seemed so minor that I didn't think that it was imperative. Needless to say, I was delighted that there was no need to reprint the pamphlet and when I announced it for sale at a price of $12.50, it sold out at once. Two years later, while visiting the Victoria and Albert Museum in London, I came upon the automaton that had been the inspiration for the poem, and I purchased one hundred and twenty-six copies—to the amazement of the clerk—to be inserted into each of the pamphlets.

Miss Moore's years back in Manhattan were, alas, marked by a steady decline in her health and energy, so I saw less and less of her, not wanting to impinge on her time or strength. Nevertheless, she retained her sense of humor. Clive Driver and his assistant Richard Talbot visited her often. She was apparently totally charmed by them, and looked forward to their visits. Her longtime maid and companion, Gladys, told me that one time Moore had said to her, "Gladys, get out my courting dress, the boys are coming."

As things turned out, not only did she want her archive in the Rosenbach Museum, she readily agreed to their project of recreating her sitting room *in toto*. To do this she gave them *carte blanch* to take whatever they needed or wanted. This caused quite a lot of hard feelings with her family, as this meant that heirloom pieces would go to Philadelphia, irrevocably.

After a lingering illness, Moore died shortly after 11 a.m. on February 5, 1972, attended by two nurses and the ever-faithful Gladys. Driver was summoned at once, and after the body had been removed, he had the apartment sealed to prevent depredation. Earlier there had been an unpleasant event when she discovered her inscribed copy of *The Waste Land* missing. Then, after she mentioned its disappearance to the person whom she suspected of having taken it, she found it replaced upside down, apparently hurriedly. After that she had the locks changed, to the consternation of the culprit, who complained to her that her keys didn't work. Without looking up from her typing, Moore replied, "They're not supposed to."

Since her death occurred on Saturday, the full-page obituary in the *Times* did not get into the early edition, distributed late Saturday night. This is the one most New Yorkers buy on their way home from their various Saturday night outings. The result of this was that her funeral was very sparsely attended, since most people did not learn of her death until after the funeral service, which took place at her lifelong place of worship, the Lafayette Avenue Presbyterian Church in Brooklyn. Obviously a large number of people had been expected, for several pews had been roped off for friends and colleagues, who failed to appear solely out of ignorance of her death.

At the time I was shocked not to see Auden, but later I learned that he was out of town. The only poets present were Elizabeth Bishop, Laura Benet, and Ned O'Gorman. Lincoln Kirstein, Monroe Wheeler, Glenway Wescott and Jeff Kindley, her protégé, completed the literary group. The only other notable present was Maurice Sendak, her neighbor and admirer. There were only a few floral tributes, although there was one marked simply "Ezra." I later learned that he had arranged a memorial service in Venice to take place at the exact same time as the Brooklyn service. At it he read some of her poems, breaking his self-imposed silence for the only time—no small tribute.

But of all of my memories of her, the one I cherish most is the luncheon she once served while still living in Brooklyn. I arrived precisely at the appointed hour to find her standing in her doorway. As the elevator door opened, she said, "Mr. Wilson, I'm in despair."

"Why, what's the matter, Miss Moore?"

"I wanted to take you to Gage and Tollner's for lunch, but when I telephoned just now to make a reservation, I found out that they don't serve lunch on Saturdays, and there was no time to go out and buy something. I didn't want you to arrive and find a note on the door saying 'Back in five minutes', so I'm afraid we'll have to make do with what I can find in the refrigerator."

I tried to reassure her that it didn't matter and that perhaps we could go somewhere else, but apparently she had made up her mind. I thought fleetingly of one of her remarks to a friend of mine to whom she had imparted the Irish way of preparing an economical meal by dropping an egg and a potato into a pot of boiling water, explaining, "When the egg is hard, the potato is soft and the meal is ready."

I also thought somewhat ruefully that it would really have been nice to possess a note saying, "Back in five minutes—Marianne Moore."

Once inside she gave me the latest issue of *The Virginia Quarterly Review* to read while she prepared lunch. Both she and Robert Frost had new poems in that particular issue. In fact his became world famous when he read it at President Kennedy's inauguration. Hers, of course, had acquired a multitude of revisions in her spidery hand.

Very shortly she reappeared from the kitchen bearing two identical trays, which we were to place in our laps. Obviously she had sorted through the refrigerator and divided everything she had found into equal portions. Each tray held the following: a cheese glass filled with heated tomato juice (not tomato soup, but heated tomato juice); a tuna salad sandwich; half a peeled apple; two wedges of gruyere cheese, still in their silver foil wrappers; a small dish of canned pears; a small dish of salted nuts; a slightly withered tangerine; and two chocolate petits fours. To supplement this she placed a large bowl of Fritos on a small table between us, saying," Eat lots of these, they are very nutritional."

As every visitor can testify, you never left her apartment without being given something to take along with you. When I left she handed me a large brown paper bag. I could scarcely wait for the elevator door to close so that I could open it to look inside. Apparently she had feared that she had not given me enough to eat, for in the bag were four items: two pecan taffy buns, a tube of anchovy paste, and the corrected copy of *The Virginia Quarterly Review.*

Now there is a somewhat amusing coda to this account of the luncheon. I published it in one of the Phoenix's Christmas pamphlets which I sent to favored customers and my circle of poet acquaintances, among whom was Donald Hall. A few years later he asked permission to use it in a book he was editing, *The Oxford Book of Literary Anecdotes.* I readily assented, only to be rather disappointed when the book appeared to find no acknowledgment of the source of the account. But I have to say that I was more grievously disappointed when three years later Donald Hall published his own autobiography, in which he described the luncheon as having been served to HIM!

Fernanda Pivano

One of the most important figures in the history of the Beat movement is a woman who is virtually unknown to most Americans, even those who are students of the era, that is, aside from the poets themselves who all acknowledge how important she was during the early period. I am referring to Fernanda Pivano, affectionately known simply as "Nanda." She almost single-handedly introduced the entire panoply of postwar American Beats to the European continent. Born in Genoa, she grew up during the Fascist period, learning English from the distinguished Italian writer Cesare Pavese, who also introduced her to such poets as Walt Whitman and Edgar Lee Masters. During World War II Pivano translated and attempted to publish Masters' *Spoon River Anthology,* however the galleys were seized by the Fascist authorities and the book suppressed. Nothing daunted, she signed a contract with the would-be publishers to translate Hemingway's masterpiece, *A Farewell to Arms.* At the time the Nazis were in control of Italy, and she was jailed for this effort. Luckily the Germans were routed from Italy before she suffered too much deprivation in jail. After the war, when Hemingway learned of this, he sent her an invitation to visit him. At first she thought that it was a practical joke by one of her friends, and ignored the letter, but when a second invitation arrived, she decided to respond. She was dazzled by the breadth of his knowledge, but not enough to accept his invitation to sleep with him.

The war over, she went back to translating other American classics, notably Fitzgerald's *The Great Gatsby* and Faulkner's *Intruders in the Dust.* Faulkner also fell for her beauty and charm, and apparently made repeated passes, but once again she refused, finding him a bore. She was then married to an architect, Ettore Sotsass, with whom she began publishing handsome quarto editions in holograph facsimile of various poets' handwriting, including titles by Corso, McClure, Whalen, and Ferlinghetti.

It was through these books that I first became acquainted with Nanda and her husband. On a trip to the United States to meet many of the poets she had championed and also to find a way of distributing the books, the couple inevitably showed up one night at the Phoenix. Against my well-established policy of *not* acting as a distributor (since the necessary book-keeping and shipping of orders were never worth the time and trouble) I was happy to make this an exception. The books were handsomely produced, they could be obtained nowhere else, and, of course, like everyone else I succumbed to Nanda's personal charm.

While they were in the shop Nanda asked if there was a bathroom she could use. I was immediately terribly embarrassed. The only one available was a public one in the hall, used by other tenants in the building, and far from clean. I explained to Nanda that while there was one, it was very primitive. Totally undaunted she replied, "What I intend to do in it is also very primitive."

She and Ettore then asked if they might see my personal collection of Beat materials, since, necessarily, the greater majority of such often ephemeral publications were manifestly unobtainable in Italy. I lived at that time at the northern end of Manhattan Island, and during the long journey uptown I was very surprised at how shocked she and her husband were by one of the subway ads promoting a hemorrhoid product. Apparently such intimate matters were not a subject of public notice in Italy. But of course most of our conversation was about the poets, among them Gregory Corso. She started laughing as she told me on an incident after his first reading in Italy where she had read her translations for the audience. At the conclusion of the reading, Gregory propositioned her. Of course, she refused him. But what had amused her was his ploy, telling her that she would go down in history as the mistress of a great and famous poet. Nanny's reply was, "Gregory, *caro,* why should I sleep with you when I have refused Hemingway and Faulkner?"

In 1964 her landmark anthology *Poesis degli Ultimi Americani* appeared, long before most Americans had even heard the names of the poets, let alone read anything by any of them. Nanda had translated some of the poems, written brief biographies of the poets, provided introductory matter and edited the volume. It is still amazing today for the early 1960s. Not one important name was overlooked. Italian readers were introduced to Bremser, Corso, Creeley, di Prima, Dorn, Duncan, Ferlinghetti, Ginsberg, Jones, Kaufman, Kelly, Kerouac, Koch, Lamantia, Levertov, Loewinsohn, McClure, O'Hara, Olson, Oppenheimer, Orlovsky (who had yet to publish a book), Sanders, Snyder, Welch, Whalen, Wieners, and Jonathan Williams. And one who must have been somewhat surprised by the company in which he found himself, Norman Mailer. Nanda continued her work on behalf of these poets, her efforts culminating in a superbly printed translation by her of Allen Ginsberg's *Sunflower Sutra.*

Although it has been two decades since I last saw Nanda, the impression she made on me is still as vivid as it was that first night. Her keenness of intellect, her wit and charm, her physical beauty, and her impeccable good taste in all matters combined to form one of the most delightful persons it has been my good fortune to meet.

Seeing Shelley Plain

In the City of Aldus

My belief that the quality of the work of Ezra Pound and his lifetime of helping other poets get established, especially T.S. Eliot and Louis Zukofsky, far overrode any questions of treason or anti-Semitism, and caused me not only to collect his work personally, but also to carry it in stock whenever possible. I had been introduced to his work by Marshall Clements at the end of the 1950s. This was a great time to collect Pound, since he was still incarcerated in St. Elizabeth's Hospital in Washington D.C., and the renaissance of his literary reputation had not yet begun. Consequently, material was available, and at very moderate prices.

But sometimes Pound entries in the Phoenix catalogs brought unusual results. I had bought Marshall's Pound collection when he decided to go to Europe for an extended stay. In this collection was a microfilm of the wartime radio broadcasts which formed the basis for the treason charges brought against him at the end of World War II. These had been monitored by the U.S. Department of Justice and transcribed from short-wave broadcasts.

As we all know, he was never brought to trial, being deemed mentally unfit to stand trial. I won't go into the legal, ethical and moral quagmires surrounding this. Virtually no one in the United States heard these broadcasts, and the text of them had never been published. So when the Library of Congress offered for sale a roll of microfilm containing the text of every broadcast, Marshall ordered one for his collection, but had no way of reading it. I suggested that we could probably make legible enlargements in my makeshift photographic darkroom, which was nothing more elaborate than my kitchen with the window blacked out with a large black plastic trash bag. So we embarked on this project, producing a few pages every week when we didn't devote the time to other diversions. While we never completed the series, we did print enough to realize that not only were the broadcasts very questionable as to treasonable content, they were incredibly garbled and inaccurate. The transcribers had no knowledge of literature in general, let alone Pound's works, making horrendous errors that any freshman high school student could have corrected.

I duly catalogued the microfilm and was astonished to receive nearly two dozen orders for it. These I was able to fill in a very short time simply by ordering more copies from the Library of Congress. Not long after the catalog had run its usual six weeks before orders stopped coming in, I was startled to receive a letter from an attorney representing "The Committee for Ezra Pound." This was the legal entity set up to handle Pound's affairs because the Justice Department, when finally dropping the charges and releasing him, had deemed Pound incompetent to manage his own affairs. This was despite the fact that in 1949 another branch of government, the Library of Congress, had awarding him its prestigious honor, the Bollingen Prize for poetry, for his volume *The Pisan Cantos,* written during his incarceration in a wire cage in the broiling midsummer Italian sun. The awarding of this prize, honoring the best American poetry issued the previous year, caused a literary furor which has no place in this narrative.

In any event, the lawyer's letter stated that I was infringing Pound's copyright in selling these transcripts. This puzzled me greatly, for the United States copyright laws very clearly held the publisher liable for copyright infringement, not any individual vendor. and in this case, the publisher was the branch of the U.S. Government charged with protecting copyrights, namely, the Library of Congress itself. I replied promptly, pointing out this discrepancy in their claim of copyright infringement. The lawyer wrote back and said that he was aware of this and added, rather plaintively, that he was simply trying to stem the flow! I sent one more letter stating that out of my regard for Pound I would cease offering them for sale.

A few years later, a similar event occurred. Ed Sanders, the publisher of the notorious underground magazine *FUCK YOU/a magazine of the arts* (a saga which is discussed in another chapter) got hold of the text of some unpublished *Cantos* and issued them in the format of a mimeographed pamphlet with stiff covers. Of course I carried them in the shop, and in fact had purchased most of the edition of three hundred copies. And once again I received a complaint about the infringement of copyright. But this time, instead of coming from the attorney, it came from Pound's principal publisher, Jay Laughlin, the founder of New Directions. He suggested that I should pay Pound royalties. I pointed out to him that as a publisher himself he knew very well who was responsible for paying royalties. He rather lamely confessed that of course he knew this, but had been unable to locate the publisher. This seemed odd to me, for Sanders was well known in the Village and in literary circles, and in fact was operating a shop of his own a few blocks away from New Directions' headquarters.

In any event, the price of the booklet was a mere two dollars. At that point I had sold perhaps twenty copies. I replied that out of my admiration for Ezra, I would this time send a check, but only on the express condition that it be recognized as being done out of admiration, not obligation. This seemed to satisfy everyone, and nothing more was ever heard about copyright violations. Some few years later another selection from the radio broadcasts was issued in Amsterdam, and I often wondered whether Laughlin and the lawyers tried to pursue the matter overseas, but felt that it was probably better not to bring the subject to their attention.

Having always tried to get my personal copies signed by their authors, starting as far back as the late 1930s long before it became the rage that it now is, I wrote to Pound at Schloss Brunnenberg in the Tyrol, where he had gone to live with his daughter Mary de Rachewiltz upon his release from St. Elizabeth's. I asked if I might send some of the small pamphlets issued by his Italian publisher, Vanni Scheiwiller, to be inscribed. Back came a polite letter from Mrs. Pound asking me not to send anything "as we are inconveniently far from the post-office" and enclosing a recent photo of Ezra. So of course, I sent nothing.

It was not until several years later that I learned that Mrs. Pound was concealing what for her must have been a painful and embarrassing situation. Ezra had decamped shortly after arriving back in Italy, and had gone off to Venice to live with Olga Rudge, his longtime companion and mother of his daughter, now the Princess de Rachewiltz. One can only admire Dorothy Pound's stoicism as well as Mary's kindness in supporting Mrs. Pound until the end of her life.

Not long after this, Pound went into his self-imposed silence, not speaking publicly except for his tribute to Marianne Moore at the time of her funeral. It was an extraordinary gesture, and whenever I think of it, I am also reminded that once, in an extremely personal revelation, Moore showed me a letter she had received from Pound saying, "You are an old man's darling."

I had always hoped to get his Venice address so that I could get a few things signed, but it was a fairly well-guarded secret, and it was not until after his death that I finally learned it. Thus it was that I was finally able to visit his home and spend an entire day with Olga Rudge. Prior to that I had written to her asking if she might have, still, a copy of a pamphlet she had caused to be issued in 1948 entitled *If This Be Treason...* containing the text of five of the controversial radio speeches. She wrote back that she might have a spare, however had never sold one, but she would let me know if she ever decided to do so. It was a gracious refusal and I did not persist. Luckily I was able eventually to procure one in the rare book market.

Then came the summer of 1982 when I was spending a few weeks in the Tyrol in the company of my close friend Kenneth Doubrava. On looking at the map I realized that we sere not far from Venice, and, in fact, could get there quickly on the *Rapido* from Innsbruck. Although I had twice visited Venice, Kenneth had never seen any of Italy, so we made plans to go. At the last minute I wrote to Miss Rudge asking if we might pay her a visit, and sent her the name and address of our hotel, just off the Piazza San Marco.

We arrived late in the afternoon, and to my astonishment when we checked in the desk clerk handed me two letters—an airmail from my business partner at the Phoenix, and one unstamped letter addressed in a large, bold hand. Flipping it over, my pulse quickened when I read the return address headed "O. Rudge." Opening it quickly there in the lobby, I was further astonished to read that while she did not want to venture out in the hot late-July sun in Venice, she would be pleased to offer us lunch at her house, concluding the letter with her telephone number. Still not quite believing what I had just read, I telephoned immediately, and somehow the erratic Venetian telephone system worked without a hitch, for there was Miss Rudge on the phone. The next day was not convenient, but the day after that would be, and an appointment was made for one p.m.

For the next day and a half I dutifully showed Ken the usual sights, including the Bridge of Sighs, the Doge's Palace, the Duomo, many of the art galleries, and the glass shops filled with the most gaudy, tasteless and vulgar objects we had seen anywhere. We were appalled that Venetian glass, treasured for centuries as the finest and most exquisite in the world, could have sunk so low. Finally the day and hour of our visit arrived, and we set out, buying a small plant on our way. I wanted to arrive exactly at the appointed hour, so as not to miss one possible minute of time that could be spent in the house where Pound had lived, or in talking with his lifetime inamorata.

The house was in the older, non-tourist section of Venice behind the Church of Santa Maria della Salute. It was in a tiny passageway just off a small connecting canal, which I had trouble locating on our map. I knew we were somewhere in the vicinity and stopped to look at the map again. A Venetian saw us, and immediately pointed to the next corner. Obviously the only Americans who came this way were those looking for the Pound-Rudge establishment. And of course there it was.

The passageway—not a street because it was a cul-de-sac—was too narrow for me to back off far enough to photograph the doorway, even with a wide-angle lens. So I lifted up the lion's-head door knocker and let it fall twice upon the dark green wooden door, wondering as I did how many other pilgrims and what assortment of great names had done likewise. Very promptly the door was opened, and there stood a white-haired lady of medium height, with blue-gray eyes, clad in a beige tailored blouse and skirt, and wearing two strands of very large glass beads. This, of course, was Olga Rudge.

The first thing she said floored me completely—"I've been reading your book; it was lent me by an English friend." I had never expected her to know that I had written one, let alone pay me the compliment of reading it. I promised then and there to send her a copy of her own. Then she added, "Come in—mind that," pointing to an upright marble slab about six inches high across the threshold. "That's to keep out the high water." With that we were in a tiny vestibule that barely held the three of us. She led the way into the main room of the house, and aside from a closet-sized kitchen running across the narrow front of the house, the only other room on the ground floor. In fact, each of the three floors were similar in layout.

The building was of either late seventeenth- or early eighteenth-century construction, and was a typical "Holy Ghost" house: i.e., one room on each floor, being named "Father," "Son," and "Holy Ghost" in ascending order. The ground floor had a large fireplace raised a couple of feet above floor level to protect it from the apparently frequent high-water flooding which, alas, are becoming more frequent as Venice sinks slowly but inexorably into the Adriatic. This fireplace was formerly used for cooking as well as heating the house. On either side of it was a small highly placed window, glazed with little lemon-colored panes. Below these were bookshelves, holding mostly recent paperbacks.

A stairway occupied the left-hand wall, and the other two walls had glass-fronted bookshelves up to shoulder height, set into the walls to keep them from projecting too far into the rather small room. Against the staircase and the wall separating the room from the entrance hall were two built-in benches extending along two sides of the table which was permanently anchored to the brick floor. The ceiling was fairly low, with closely spaced dark natural wood beams.

On the very high mantelpiece lay two life masks, one of Pound and one of her. I asked her when they had been cast, and she replied that she though it might have been about 1929. Aside from the bookcases, the only

With Olga Rudge, Venice

other objects in the room were a couple of framed photos of EP plus the famous Wyndham Lewis pen-and-ink sketch of Pound. There was also a small Gaudier-Brzeska statuette of two elongated figures with what looked like halos. Much as I wanted to, there was no opportunity of examining the contents of the bookcases, although I could spot one of the early New Directions annuals (Volume 3) and a Greek translation of Pound.

Miss Rudge went into the kitchen briefly, and when she returned, lunch was served almost immediately by an Italian maid. It was superb, consisting of delicious prosciutto and melon, followed by a risotto, delicately sautéed yellow peppers, a salad, and an excellent chilled white wine and to close, mixed fruit tarts with espresso.

She was, by her own admission, a nonstop talker. Originally from Youngstown, Ohio, and half-Irish by descent (the middle name is O'Connell), her conversation was frequently punctuated—perhaps every third sentence— with an interrogatory *"Capito?"* or alternately, "You do understand what I mean?", although she really never paused long enough to get an answer.

At first the drift of the conversation, or perhaps more accurately, the monologue, was difficult to follow, for she was intent on elaborating on her displeasure with a group of people making a documentary film about Pound for which she had offered background material ultimately not used. This was doubtless what eventually appeared in a PBS series on poets of the twentieth century under the collective title *Voices and Visions.* However at the time I had not been aware of the project, and was thus somewhat at sea as to the references.

Gradually, whenever possible, I tried to steer the conversation closer to the subject of Pound himself where I would be in somewhat more familiar waters. At last she took up this thread and then started on a vigorous denunciation of what she regarded as the deliberate falsification of many of the facts of Pound's career, claiming that people who ought to know better repeated outright lies. She was, however, canny enough not to identify them too closely.

When lunch was finished she said that she would like to show us the rest of the house, "But it is a mess," she explained. We both protested that it did not matter, and so with very little persuasion she took us up to the second floor, which contained a bathroom and two small bedrooms, one of which, behind a closed door, had been Ezra's. She opened this door just long enough for us to have a peek in. There was a tiny iron-framed single bed close to the wall, along which was a low bookshelf crammed with books. Regrettably, there wasn't enough time to examine than closely, for I'd have loved to know what books Pound kept by his bedside. But very touchingly, on the pillow lay a copy of *Personae*. It was interesting to me that it was not *The Cantos*. I have since wondered if that was an indication of Pound's own favorite part of his work, or if it was Olga's.

On the outer side of the door was a large poster from the 1920s announcing a concert by Georg Antheil and Olga Rudge. This had been arranged by Pound, and was the beginning of the liaison between her and Pound. She picked up a recent recording by Antheil and asked if I had ever listened to it. When I replied that I had, she wanted to know what I thought of it. Giving her an honest answer I said, "Well, sometimes I was amused and sometimes bored." She agreed with this, but then said she had been more bored than amused. Kenneth then asked her about some of the more technical aspects of playing the violin. I hoped that this might lead to her demonstrating her answers, but she demurred, saying she had not picked up the instrument for too many years.

We then proceeded to the top—"Holy Ghost"—floor. It was spacious and well lighted, airy, with very little furniture: a studio couch, two small chairs, and a large wicker chair with a high round back, which I immediately recognized as the very one in which I had seen Pound seated in several photos from his last years. She had tied a yellow ribbon across the seat to prevent anyone from sitting in it—but whether from practical or sentimental reasons I never discovered. On the wall over the studio couch was an enormous enlargement of an early map of Venice, also prominent in many of the late photos of Pound.

We sat there for the remainder of the afternoon as she warmed to the subject of the misrepresentation of Pound's activities. First of all, she broached the subject of his silence for the last decade of his life. She claimed that he was always silent, a statement that was rather difficult to reconcile with all that I had previously read and heard about his long-standing reputation as a raconteur, advisor and teacher. Nevertheless, she supported this statement with an anecdote in which she said that she had once taken Pound to a party given by some friends of hers who did not know him. The next day one of them remarked, "Your friend is very strange: the whole evening he spoke only to the dog." Perhaps it was Pound's subtle comment on the intellectual caliber of the other guests!

Next she tackled the oft-repeated and firmly held belief that upon returning to Italy Pound had given the Fascist salute from the deck of the ship as it docked. I had to admit that I had seen the widely printed photo in the newspapers and had believed this to be true. Miss Rudge, however vehemently denied that it was a salute of any sort, but merely an ordinary joyous wave of the hand to a group of friends and well-wishers welcoming him on the pier, and that the photographer had caught the moment with his hand in motion. She said that there were many of that welcoming party still alive who could corroborate her statement that it was not a Fascist salute.

If you examine the photo carefully, you can see that Pound is laughing and is not as serious as someone probably would be if giving such salute. Later on, in the privacy of my hotel room, I experimented in front of the mirror and saw that indeed, in a quick photo of someone waving, an upraised arm could easily resemble a Fascist salute if the action were frozen at its zenith. Knowing how the media would jump at such a thing I finally concluded that Rudge was probably correct. I also met briefly that evening one of my customers who had been in the group on the pier, and posed the question to him. He wholeheartedly supported Rudge's contention that the currently held theory is based on a canard. A newsreel of the event could quickly and easily prove her claim, but none seems to have been made.

She then moved into the touchy subject of Pound's anti-Semitism, the most lingering of the charges against him. "Oh, of course he used the word 'kike,'" she admitted, "but that was simply common parlance of the time." Of course that does not excuse his insensitivity. However his entire literary circle and many outside of the circle—Hemingway, Eliot, Wyndham Lewis and other such notables—regularly resorted to such expressions in their speech and correspondence in those pre-politically correct days. But Pound alone has been singled out for his usage.

However objectionable his written references are, such usage remained with him only a literary stance. It was never carried over into practice, for he had many long-term friendships with Jewish writers. In fact, he used a considerable amount of his time promoting their careers, especially those of George Oppen and Louis Zukovsky, the latter of whom stated often that he never in all their long friendship detected any anti-Semitism whatever.

I mentioned this to Miss Rudge. She nodded in agreement, but then lamented that Zukovsky had pulled his punch by adding that he was sorry that Pound had never mentioned Auschwitz or Dachau. "The point here," she continued, "is that we simply did not know about these until the war was over." It is also a matter of record that Pound spoke out against pogroms.

Later in the afternoon she mentioned her grandson Walter de Rachewiltz, now grown and married, with a son of his own. She was very pleased that he had given the child "Ezra" for his middle name. She was also proud of the fact that Walter had also become an author in his own right, following in both his father's and grandfather's footsteps—albeit in the field of history—and had written *Brot im Tirol,* a history of the making of bread in the Tyrol region where he was brought up. At this point the conversation drifted away from Pound, and she wanted us to know how grateful she was to Count Chigi, who gave her employment during the difficult years of Pound's incarceration.

By now it was getting late in the day, nearly five p.m., and we were due back at the hotel at six for a supper date with an acquaintance. Still, we had difficulty finding an opening in the conversation that would give us reason to depart. Eventually we did start down the steps when it occurred to me that I would like to see the Gaudier profile sketch that had been used as a frontispiece in so many of Pound's books, and even for some years on his personal stationery. She replied that Pound had given it, along with a Gaudier statuette, to the Museé de l'Art Moderne in Paris, adding that he carried them to the museum in his own hands. "Pound never sold anything; he always gave." By then we were at the doorway, where she agreed to pose for some photos.

On the way back to the hotel, we made the inevitable wrong turn, something almost impossible not to do in Venice. But it seemed, after all, that Pound's spirit must have been guiding our steps, for there, looking exactly as it must have a half-century ago, was the boatyard Pound celebrated in *Canto LVI,* "where Ogni Santi meets San Trovaso."

Visiting Laura Riding

By all accounts, Laura Riding has been one of the most intriguing writers of the twentieth century. But many critics have labeled her "difficult." This adjective refers not only to her work, but more especially to her personality. Less kind critics and biographers—especially those concerned with Robert Graves—have not hesitated to document in painful detail what they claim was her tendency to manipulate, and her self-aggrandizement. While a Graves biographer is obviously not an impartial judge, Riding's actions would seem to give some credence to a portion of the charges leveled against her. But in all fairness, it should be noted that no one has published her side of the matter.

My own assessment of her personality is based on the opportunities I had in the Phoenix Book Shop of reading various series of correspondences. They followed, in every case, the same pattern. The exchange would open with great friendliness on her part, and after varying lengths of time, Miss Riding, or Mrs. Jackson, as she insisted on being called for the last three decades of her life, would take umbrage at some remark, and would terminate the correspondence with a verbal barrage that quite often left the poor recipient wondering what on earth he had said or done to provoke such a storm.

Then one day in the winter of 1981 I was startled to receive a telephone call from the lady herself. I was immediately charmed by the extreme musicality of her voice along with her apparent amiability. It seemed that she wanted to sell some of her manuscripts and had become dissatisfied with the dealer who had been handling such transactions up to that point. She told me right off who he was and I immediately went on guard, for he was well known to me and I had only the highest regard for him. She wanted me to handle such sales from now on. I gulped, but agreed to do so, thinking to myself, "Well, it won't last, but at least it will go once around."

Before I could ask how she had decided to come to me, she told me that I had been recommended by her friend Ted Wilentz. Ted and I had been acquainted for many years, from his days as co-owner with his brother of the famous Eighth Street Bookshop just a few streets way from mine. Then we came to the problem of how to ship such a bulky and valuable lot. As it happened, I had planned a vacation trip to Florida, where she was living, right after Christmas and rashly suggested that I could visit her and bring them back with me. This seemed to be a practical solution and she gave me her phone number so I could call her when I got to Florida and receive directions how to reach her.

By the time I did get there, I was cursing myself for having volunteered to do this, for I had not known exactly where Wabasso was in relation to Hollywood, where I would be staying. It was well up the coast, some two hundred miles south of Jacksonville. It would be a three-hour drive at the very least. so I decided to phone her and tell her that it would be impossible. After screwing up my courage I placed the call. Before I could say a single word, she poured out her pleasure at the prospect, and totally disarmed me of my intention. Reluctantly I agreed, and we settled on a date.

So on January 15th off I set for the long drive, which took exactly three hours. I somehow missed the entrance to her home but realized my mistake almost at once and turned back to enter the palmetto-lined dirt driveway. Suddenly there I was confronting a two-storied white frame house with a citrus orchard behind it—certainly not looking like the lair of a reputed dragon-lady. Beside the house was an open-sided packing shed, no longer used as I was soon to find out. she and her husband, the late Schuyler Jackson, had for some time run a citrus shipping business, but since his death she no longer operated this, and now had reduced her holdings to ten acres.

I got out of the car and went up to the screen door, only to find it locked. However she had seen me drive up and was hobbling to the door. (Decades before she had become badly crippled by her fall from a third-story flat in London.) She was short and stooped, her face lined, and crowned with a great aureole of feathery white hair held in place by a narrow black velvet ribbon. And shining out of this was a pair of the most brilliant blue eyes

I've ever encountered. Extending her hand, she apologized for its coldness (it was abnormally cold in Florida then—in fact it was the first time in history that there was snow in every one of the forty-eight contiguous states.)

We went inside. At first I couldn't see anything due to the sudden transition from the brilliant sunlight to the very dark wood-paneled room. Though a very large room, it had only two small windows on either side of the door. As I later found out, there was a bedroom on each side of the room; these were much cheerier, being painted white. There was also a treacherous looking staircase without a railing leading upstairs, but this was closed off by a door at the top, and I never saw what the second story consisted of. We proceeded into a second room, obviously the main one, again large, and this time running the entire width of the house. It contained a small and apparently seldom used fireplace. I thought that the day was certainly ideal for a fire, but of course it would have been awkward for her to have managed to lay a fire on her own, crippled as she was. There were two easy chairs in this room, plus two desks and a dining room table pushed against the wall below two large windows through which came brilliant sunshine and a small amount of heat. Beyond this was a large, old-fashioned kitchen.

She gave me some coffee, much needed after the chilly three-hour drive. Sitting down side by side at the dining table, we started going over the manuscripts. Almost at once she decided that perhaps we had better start lunch. She went into the kitchen and took out a quart of ice cream from an insulated chest, only to find that it had completely melted and was pouring all over the floor. She had not realized that such chests had to be packed with ice. Then her telephone rang, and I took over cleaning up the mess while she went to answer it. Finally, the cold lunch was ready and we sat at opposite ends of the table in the very welcome warmth coming in from the sunshine. Once again I noted the bushy white hair, the wrinkled face and the piercing blue eyes, making a startling resemblance to Einstein.

I had brought with me a bottle of Riesling, and dared mention the fact that at first I had selected in the wine shop a Graves, but had thought it would be a poor choice to bring.

"Because the name might have been unwelcome?" she questioned lightly, then going on to say that she of course knew of it during her time with Robert Graves since his younger Brother had referred to Robert as *"Graves Superieur."*

There was a bright yellow curtain hanging in the doorway behind her, and with the light coming in from the window, I was struck with the Vermeer-like quality of the scene. I asked to take some photos. She was very reluctant to allow me to do so, having had an unpleasant experience recently with one photographer who had wanted to take close-up portraits, saying with remarkable lack of tact that the lines in her face revealed "so much wonderful pain." Finally she agreed to let me take just one, but from a distance, and for myself alone. In the event, I did not capture the Vermeer quality I had wanted and I kept my word, sending her the negative along with a print for herself.

While she was busy preparing the lunch, she invited me to look about, and of course I went first to the bookshelves. I saw almost nothing but recent paperbacks, and asked her where the others, her own books, might be. She replied that she did not have many books and had been "faulted for having so few." She went on to say that Graves had kept the entire library when he returned to Majorca after the war. In fact, the only item of collector interest that I could see on her shelves was a set of hardbound *Epilogue* magazines. What surprised me was the large number of mathematical journals, and even more surprising, almost all of the great fantasy books for children—Tolkien, the "Oz" books, the "Alice" books, *The Wind in the Willows,* etc.

I queried her about the proper pronunciation of the famous Seizin press that she and Graves had run on Majorca, and was told that it was pronounced "season." I told her that I owned some Seizin editions, and she wanted to know which ones. This gave me the opportunity to bring up Gertrude Stein.

"Yes, it had been a nice friendship, but gradually Gertrude's letters were devoted exclusively to her dog, Basket, and that seemed a waste of time to me, so I let the correspondence drop." She agreed with me that Alice Toklas had been the more interesting person. I asked her what became of all the letters, and she said she had given them all to Cornell, emphasizing, "I never sell letters."

We went back to sorting the manuscripts while I made notes to identify them, an especially necessary task as her handwriting was difficult at best and even the typescripts were heavily emended in the nearly indecipherable script. Coupled with this was her extremely idiosyncratic syntax,

Laura Riding

and her love of hyphenated compounds, making decipherment truly a problem, especially for a reader like me who was not totally familiar with her *oeuvre.* She had asked me during our initial phone conversation to bring some file folders, since the cold weather had prevented her fro going to town to fetch any. When I placed them on the table she asked, "May I cover that? Will you let me pay for them?" When I demurred, she smiled and said, "I didn't think you would."

As we continued the sorting I mentioned that of course I would offer the manuscripts to Lola Szladits, the director of the Berg Collection at the New York Public Library. When I said that Lola had asked me to convey her love, Laura replied that she liked Lola, but then added, "We did have a disagreement—did she tell you?"

Lola had told me about it, but I decided to feign ignorance, and replied, "No, Lola is very discreet."

"Oh well, we've made up now. It was all simply because she has trouble with English."

This amazed me, for Dr. Szladits had an impeccable command of English, seldom equaled by most native-born Americans. I did not want to stir up a controversy, and so sidestepped the issue by saying, truthfully,

"Well, English is not her native language." Laura immediately wanted to know what it was, apparently not aware of the fact that Lola was Hungarian.

By this time we had finished sorting the manuscripts and had placed them in two cartons. It was getting late, and I wanted to start the long drive back, but my departure was delayed when Laura decided to give me two large sacks of grapefruit and oranges that she had picked the day before to save them from the severe frost. I took these all out to the car, and on my return she gave me a copy of *The Telling* and the new edition of her *Collected Poems*, both very affectionately inscribed. While she was making her way to the door with me, we briefly discussed mutual acquaintances in New York, such as Ben Sonnenburg (who had been the caller during the ice cream debacle) and she was surprised to learn that he, too, was physically impaired; Sonia Raiziss; and a certain David Giannini, for whom I expressed immediate dislike. She then confided that he had at one time bad-mouthed both Gotham and Phoenix, but that ultimately she realized that she should disregard these statements. Finally, it came time to leave. At the very last she confided to me that the next day was her birthday.

On the long ride back I had time to reflect on the day's visit. It had turned out to be totally unlike my preconceptions. Laura riding had been one of the most charming persons I had ever met. Had it not been for the long ride I would gladly have stayed on and on. I could easily see how she held sway over her circle in the '20s and '30s.

When I returned, taking my cue from her confidence to me, I sent her a birthday gift that I though she needed against the really oppressive cold in her house—a combination quilted affair that could be used to sit in, akin to a sleeping bag, but which also unzipped to make a flat quilt for the bed. This charmed her so that I received no less than three letters discussing it. Later on I also sent her a small box of candied grapefruit peel, made by my friend Kenneth Doubrava from the grapefruit she had given me.

Thus a friendship began which endured against all odds, to judge from her correspondences of years past to others that I had seen. As a special mark of her affection, I was told to address her simply as "Laura." And furthermore, she always remembered my birthday. On one such, she presented me—with apologies for not being able to get out to purchase something nicer—the four-page holograph manuscript of the last poem she had written, still unpublished! What could she possibly have bought that would have been nicer?

Delmore Schwartz

In 1967 I received a telephone call from an elderly lady in the Bronx who identified herself as the aunt of Delmore Schwartz, asking me if I could come and appraise his library and manuscripts for sale. This was shortly after his death in 1966. A date was set and I journeyed uptown to that once elegant part of the Bronx, now sadly run down, and becoming a virtual slum. I looked forward to seeing a potentially fascinating and valuable collection of books and papers.

Schwartz had burst upon the poetry scene in 1938 with his first book *In Dreams Begin Responsibilities* which garnered perhaps the most rapturous reviews ever to greet a debut book. Unfortunately, Schwartz's work did not live up to the promise of this initial effort, and by the time the great flowering of American poetry in the postwar world began to manifest itself, he had produced little more that was well received by the public, and was virtually forgotten. He drifted into alcoholism and eventually died in a seedy Times Square hotel.

I had hoped that his library, at least, had been preserved, as it should have had some interesting presentation copies from his peers of the prewar days. But apparently all such books must have been converted to cash to meet his needs, for when I was shown his entire library, it consisted of a mere one hundred thirty books, of which most were paperback reprints. After making a quick survey, I suggested to the aunt that she allow me to take the lot back to the shop, along with five groups of poetry manuscripts, so that I could describe them to a potential buyer. I envisioned this being a university, which is what eventually transpired with their purchase be a major New York university.

She agreed, and so I did this. In trying to write up a description that would entice an institutional librarian, I began to get a picture of Delmore Schwartz, the man and the poet. Strangely, a sharper picture emerged from this tiny group of works than did the portraits of Marianne Moore or W.H. Auden, both of whose extensive libraries I had handled. Schwartz, living in one tiny hotel room, had concentrated his interests sharply. Whatever his state of health was, his mind remained acute, and he continued working at his chosen craft, despite his failure to produce further significant work.

First of all, there was a small group of some two dozen odd hardbound volumes of literature, ranging from the Elizabethan tragedies down to some of T.S. Eliot's criticism, notably *The Uses of Poetry and the Uses of Criticism and After Strange Gods*. The latter interestingly bore the signature of ownership and the bookplate of James Laughlin, who not only had been Schwartz's college roommate, but also his first publisher shortly after Laughlin had founded the firm of New Directions. Perhaps the only book of any collector value was a presentation copy of Norman Holmes Pearson's important *The Oxford Anthology of American Literature*. The latest item among these books was *The Collected Stories of James T. Farrell*.

Then came the balance of his literary library—sixty paperbacks, starting with Chaucer and running down through Fielding, Tolstoy, Dostoevsky, Wallace Stevens, and a nod at Plato. Most of these were annotated—sometimes quite extensively—including, surprisingly, Gertrude Stein's *Three Lives.*

As a working poet he had a surprisingly wide range of dictionaries, including the two-volume *Oxford Shorter English Dictionary* as well as French-English and German-English dictionaries, along with a rhyming dictionary and an etymological one. All bore his signature and quite often his annotations. Next came what were obviously his main interests, since these books were heavily annotated. Four were outstanding because of the wealth of their extensive annotations: *The Penguin book of French Verse* in which the section on Valery was impossible to decipher because of the density of his notations; next was Rilke's *Notebooks of Malte Brigge* along with the *Selected Poetry and Prose of Gerard Manley Hopkins;* and finally two Shakespeare plays: *Measure for Measure* and *King Lear.* While the latter is not surprising, the former is certainly an unusual choice.

But Schwartz's main passion seems to have been James Joyce. His copy of *Ulysses* was so worn as to be in imminent danger of falling apart, and his annotations were so many as to be virtually equal in bulk to Joyce's original text. The same could be said, both as to wear and as to the amount of comment, of *Finnegan's Wake*. There were also three critical works on Joyce replete with annotations: Benstock's *Joyce-Again's Wake;* Burgess' *Re-Joyce;* and Gilbert's classic, *James Joyce's Ulysses*. In addition there was what seemed to be a brand-new copy of *Dubliners*. I could only conclude that this must have been a very recent purchase, as there was not a mark on it.

Finally, there was what I would term the "human side" of Schwartz, areas other than literary that obviously fascinated him. These included such diverse items as a large "coffee table" type of book entitled *The Movies;* a book on handwriting analysis, as usual heavily annotated, and with many slips of paper with various specimens of handwriting laid in, apparently gathered from acquaintances; and somewhat amusingly, *Five Hundred Songs That Made the Hit Parade*.

Lastly, an item that was the most revealing of his interests—a copy of *Adam Film Quarterly* devoted to nudist movie scenarios. Rounding out the book collection were no less than fifteen volumes on human sexuality, all as copiously written in as the Joyce volumes, along with a large book entitled *Eros Denied* and a lavish folio of ancient Greek erotic art under the title *Eros Kalos*.

It would be pointless as well as totally unfair to Schwartz's memory to try to sort out a meaning from this concentrated group of books. One can only conclude that it showed the tragic failure of a poet blessed with a superb intellect and obvious talent who somehow, perhaps through no fault of his own, never lived up to his initial promise.

Gary Snyder

Ever since I started reading the postwar poets I had been attracted to the work of Gary Snyder. And, as always, after I had acquired a few of his earlier books I wrote and asked if I might send them to him for signing. He had, fortunately for me, recently returned from a long period of residence in Japan in one of the Buddhist monasteries in Kyoto. It was here that his first two books had been printed—*Rip-Rap* and a strange book (to most Americans, that is,) entitled *The Wooden Fish*. This is actually a phonetic translation into the Western alphabet of the manual of Buddhist rituals, made for the benefit of American aspirants who could not read Japanese. Gary was kind enough to agree, although I am not sure that it was altogether convenient for him to have to repack the books and then take them down the mountain to the post office. He was then living in a rather remote cabin in the woods.

Then, after the Oblong Octavo series was well under way, I wanted to have Gary in the series. The only signed limited he had done was in England, and in an edition severely limited to only fifty copies. I was both pleased and surprised that he readily accepted the proposition, and in 1969 he sent me the text of a recent poem entitled *The Blue Sky*. At once I sent it to the printer who finished it in early November.

For a while there was a bad period when I almost had to cancel the project. Very late in the proceedings Gary had decided that he wanted a page of explanation of the cover design, which he had supplied through his rendering of petroglyphs portraying an Indian legend. The text had already been set up to fit the number of pages required. To add an extra page at that state of the proceedings would not only have been an extra expense, it would have resulted in three blank pages in the pamphlet.

I was in some despair about this, and during a telephone conversation with my friend John Martin, the publisher of the renowned Black Sparrow books, I mentioned my quandary. John almost jumped through the telephone in his eagerness to take over the printing; apparently he had been trying unsuccessfully for several years to get Gary to allow him to publish something. The problem was finally resolved by printing the explanation in small type on the inner rear flap, a solution that was acceptable to Gary, thank goodness. Then the copies had to be signed. Usually the booklets had to be mailed to the author, but as luck would have it, Gary was scheduled to give a reading at the Ninety-second Street Y in late November. He suggested that he could sign them at that time, relieving both of us of the trouble of mailing the booklets back and forth across the continent.

Gary was staying at the home of a friend on the East Side where I met him very early on the morning of November 22, 1969. It was a truly elegant town house behind the Hotel Carlyle. I really would have liked a tour of the house, but all I saw was the foyer and the kitchen where Gary was boiling water for morning tea. Being a confirmed tea drinker, I was delighted not to have to explain that I never drank coffee and really enjoyed tea in the morning. My delight was very soon dashed. Gary was making green tea from a green powder which he stirred with something that had an uncanny likeness to my father's shaving brush. At that point his host, apparently a friend from their Kyoto days, came down and joined us. I took one sip and almost choked. It was unbearably strong—and of course I knew enough not to ask for sugar. Nevertheless, both of them rhapsodized over its excellence. Somehow I managed to drink it all down, although I nearly threw up at the first mouthful, and very thankfully accepted a bowl of "white tea," traditionally used to rinse out your bowl (an in my case, my mouth).

During this ordeal I got my first real look at Gary. He was somewhat shorter than I had expected, and spare of frame, probably five feet eight or nine at most. It's always difficult to judge height from photographs. His face was also lined more than one would expect for a man in his forties. This was doubtless the result of his passion for living in the rugged out-of-doors as much as possible. His voice was pleasing, coupled with a very direct manner, which augured a good reading. He was clad in what was then the classic norm—hippie beads, blue jeans, and mountain boots.

We then took a taxi downtown to the shop. It was a bit awkward getting a conversation going. After all, we had never met before and correspondence had been solely on business. But eventually we succeeded. I first asked if his *Mountains and Rivers Without End* indicated that this was going to be his ongoing work, since several of his peers seemed to be engaged in following the example of Pound and Williams, devoting many years to the completion of a many-volumed work.

"Good God, no!" he replied, "I don't want to spend the rest of my life tacking on bits and pieces. The way it's shaping now, I'll be done with it in two years. I've got too many other things to do."

Then I asked about his Japanese wife Masa (his second, married after he and Joanne Kyger had divorced).

"Three weeks ago it was touch and go when our son was born prematurely, weighing only three and a half pounds. But all is okay now and he'll probably be out of the hospital in a couple of weeks more."

We then got onto the subject of selling manuscripts or donating them to an institution in order to take a tax deduction. He revealed a business sense unequaled by any other poet I've ever met. And I might add, few businessmen of my acquaintance are so carefully and skillfully organized in that area. He takes depreciation not only on his typewriter, but also on his personal library, books being after all the "tools of his trade." He also has managed to take off all the expenses when he goes meditating in the desert or in the mountains. His tax accountant has proven to the government's satisfaction that such trips are research. The clincher in this argument was a poem that Gary had written after one of his mediations in the desert.

Then we arrived at the shop—the old Phoenix at 18 Cornelia Street—and as he was hungry (who wouldn't be after nothing more substantial than that god-awful so-called "tea"?) I took him to my favorite plain ordinary restaurant in the Village, Mytera's (alas long since disappeared). At my recommendation we had hamburgers and apple pie, both specialties of the house. I wasn't sure whether or not Gary was a vegetarian, but he went along with my suggestion. Over lunch he wanted to know what was happening in the poetry scene in New York. I allowed as how nothing was happening, since most of the practicing poets—Diane di Prima, Allen Ginsburg, Ted

Seeing Shelley Plain

Berrigan, Gregory Corso, John Ashbery, W.S. Merwin, Diane Wakoski—had all left town and Frank O'Hara had died. Virtually no one was left.

Having mentioned di Prima, we discussed her involvement in what she then firmly believed was the coming revolution. It must be remembered that the Vietnam War was in full swing at this time, and a very large segment of the American population, especially the younger portion of it, was seriously at odds with the government. I tried not to probe deeply, but Gary was not afraid to say that he thought it was a definite possibility, saying, "Weapons for private individuals ARE necessary."

Perhaps I should have pursued this more deeply, but I wanted to get his ideas about individual survival either in the city or in the wilderness should it come to pass. In the case of trying to live in the wilderness, I at least, felt that some cultural artifacts might be necessary to preserve sanity. He agreed wholeheartedly that some would be a necessity, recommending "A few books—very few, but thought-provoking ones. For example *The Bagavad Gita* should give you enough food tor thought for several years."

I suggested some records, since I simply can't live without music.

"But you can't depend on electricity. The important thing is to take some music-making instruments.

"But I have absolutely no talent in that line, I objected."

"Oh, it's not necessary to have the over-produced music we know of today," answered Gary, "It's amazing what you can do with just two sticks or some finger cymbals, or a simple flute if you get away from an audience and lose your self-consciousness at being heard."

I went on to add that I had serious doubts about anyone's ability to get out of New York City if strife came, and that I had already prepared for a short siege in the city, having laid in a cache of bottled water, canned food, candles, a hibachi with charcoal, etc. He immediately added, "Get some plastic bags to shit in. The water will be turned off and you won't have toilets."

It seems almost ridiculous now, but at the time it was deadly serious, and it was not too long after this that several major cities in the United States were set afire. Luckily for me, New York was not one of them.

Lunch being over, we returned to the shop for the signing. He seemed pleased with the physical appearance of the books, and duly signed them, insisting that I arrange them in strict numerical order—the only one of my authors to do so. He also signed some more books from my personal col-

184

lection, as well as inscribing a poem in the shop's guest book. Then Gary left to go back to his host's town house in order to prepare for the reading that night. It was a sellout, and the audience was in raptures. He read *The Blue Sky* to thunderous applause, after which he waved a copy of the pamphlet and said, "You can buy it tomorrow at the Phoenix Book Shop."

It sold out that very next day.

Tea With Miss Toklas

In 1958, shortly after I began collecting the works of Gertrude Stein, I was offered a small group of postcards plus a letter which she and Alice Toklas had written to Allen Tanner and Pavel Tchelitchev during Stein's first lecture tour in England in 1926. At this time the revival of interest in Stein had not yet begun, and there were only a few collectors of her *oeuvre,* a fact which was fortunate for me since prices were still modest. Although it was reasonably priced, purchasing this correspondence presented a serious financial difficulty for me since my salary during that period was equally modest. After all, how much could one earn as an "Executive Correspondent" in a cuckoo clock factory located in midtown Manhattan?

Nevertheless, at once I realized that I had to purchase these items. Not only were the Stein messages marvelously typical of her style, but an even greater pleasure were those from Alice. None of her letters had as yet been published and it was a revelation to learn that they were every bit as sprightly as those of her famous companion. In casting about to find a way to raise the money, I realized that among my World War II military souvenirs I had some Nazi material, including a genuine Hitler autograph on an army document. So I sold it along with some signatures of some minor Third Reich figures to buy some Gertrude Stein autographs (a delicious piece of irony that would have gladdened Gertrude's heart, whatever effect it might have had on Adolf's!) The more I read and re-read these miniature delights, the more I wanted somehow to publish them.

I eventually conceived the idea of issuing them as a pamphlet to be used as my Christmas greeting. Knowing that Dr. Donald Gallup at Yale was Gertrude Stein's literary executor, I sent him transcripts of the messages, and asked if he could possible allow me to have two hundred copies printed. Although I had not yet met Dr. Gallup, he was both prompt and cordial in his reply, saying he could authorize the publication of the Stein letters but that I would have to consult with Miss Toklas for her permission, and making the proviso that the edition would have to be limited to one hundred copies. I was very pleased with his reply, for I had actually expected a refusal.

At once I wrote to Miss Toklas, asking if I might call on her in Paris, as I would be accompanying my parents on their "Grand Tour" in April. I thought that it would not only be interesting to me, but that it might be a simpler and better approach. I mentioned *en passant* that one of my close friends was the widow of the sculptor Elie Nadelman, whose early work had been championed by Gertrude Stein, and who had been the subject of one of her "portraits". Miss Toklas very promptly wrote back a brief note regretting that she would not be able to receive me as she would not be in Paris in April.

To this letter I replied stating the reason for wanting to visit her. Again she replied promptly:

"Thank you so much for writing to me about Mrs.
Nadelman, as she is one of my kindest memories.
About the publication of the notes to Allen Tanner—it is
difficult to answer as I have no memory of what these notes
may have.
As you are motoring south, could you possibly bring them
with you and show them to me at Acqui Terme—Grand
Hotel Antiche-Italia—I shall be there between the 25th of
this month and the 6th of May.
Very sincerely,
Alice Toklas"

Fate, however, often plays nasty tricks, for as we approached northern Italy, both my mother and I were taken sick and had to forego the visit with Miss Toklas and press on as quickly as possible to Rome where I would be staying with my close friend, Marshall Clements (who had been instrumental in introducing me to Stein's work) and where we could receive proper medical care. So the publishing project had to be temporarily abandoned.

After returning home I sent Miss Toklas copies of the letters and received her permission to have them printed. The pamphlet eventually appeared in time for Christmas, 1959. It was entitled *On Our Way*, a phrase taken from one of Stein's postcard messages to Allen Tanner. This was the beginning of a correspondence and developing friendship which lasted until her death ten years later. Our correspondence was mostly casual, since, after all, we had not yet met and really did not have much to tell one another. On one occasion I had given an Alice Toklas Birthday Dinner at my apartment in honor of her birthday on April 30th. The menu consisted solely of items chosen from her famous cookbook. She seemed pleased when I later reported this in detail to her. In the same letter, I was brash enough to send her a recipe for chicken breasts sautéed with tomatoes, bouillon cubes and other ingredients. I should have known better! Back came the always prompt reply in her tiny, spidery hand (so thin that she must have used the point of a pin for a nib):

> "It was good of you to remember me and know that I had a
> birthday and when—and best of all to send me a recipe for
> chicken breasts sautés. We make a similar one here in Paris
> but the bouillon cube is replaced by homemade bouillon."

She concluded the letter by telling me of her plans to fly to Acqui Terme for the lava baths to relieve the arthritic pains which beset her "and then to go to Rome to stay for a week or ten days."

This trip was to prove disastrous for her. While she was away, the landlord of the rue Christine apartment invoked a new French law stipulating that anyone who remained away from an apartment for three consecutive months was considered to have abandoned it and could be evicted. Despite the fact that Alice had gone to Italy for reasons of her health, nothing availed, not even the intervention of André Malraux, at that time the French Minister of Culture. Friends found her an apartment in the fifteenth arrondisement, far from the familiar *sixieme* where she had spent most of her life, and the entire span of years with Gertrude. Poor, frail, nearly blind Alice had been evicted.

But even worse was to follow. Under Stein's crystal-clear will, everything was left to Alice in her lifetime, including the fabulous art collection.

The will specifically stated that Alice had the right to sell any or all of the collection for her own support, if necessary. After Toklas' death the collection was to pass to Stein's only nephew, Allen Stein, who had married a Romanian woman (Alice mistakenly referred to her as Armenian). The nephew had died while Alice was still living on the rue Christine. Alice had been very scrupulous about the collection. All of the funds available from Stein's estate had gone to help defray the costs of publishing all of her remaining work. This amounted to seven substantial volumes from the Yale University Press. In the first couple of decades after Stein's death there was no great interest in her work. Royalties were paltry, and the Yale edition did not sell well, and in fact, eventually had to be remaindered.

Alice lived in near poverty during this period, existing mainly on support from a small handful of loyal friends. She did sell a few Picasso drawings, but adamantly refused to break up the nucleus of the paintings. The famed Picasso portrait of Gertrude had been willed to the Metropolitan Museum in New York, but the remaining group was still intact. Allen Stein's widow apparently got tired of waiting for Alice to die, and complained that Alice was in the first place illegally selling off the collection—definitely not true—and in the second place not properly caring for a national treasure. The result of this was that the French government impounded all of the paintings pending a decision as to who was the rightful owner.

Such was the state of affairs when I finally met her face to face on my next trip to Paris in 1963. Ever the proper hostess, although not at all well, she had gotten out of bed and into an easy chair beside it, clad in a bed jacket and lap robe. I arrived punctually, armed with a couple of gifts: a carton of cigarettes, as I knew she was a heavy smoker; some fancy Japanese matches; a bottle of brandy which I knew she used at least in cooking; and a recording of some Stein pieces read by a fan named Addison Metcalf, entitled "Mother Goose in Montparnasse." It turned out that she did not possess a record player. (She later wrote to me that Joe Barry, an American correspondent who took care of some of her many needs, had brought her one so that she could listen to it.)

After we chatted briefly, she rang a bell and summoned Jacinta, her Spanish maid. She offered me a choice of what she termed "an indifferent sherry or an excellent Chinese tea." I chose the latter. When Jacinta had left the room she said, sotto voce, "You'd better see to the brewing of that yourself, Jacinta can't do anything right." So I accomplished this as best as I could—not knowing any Spanish and Jacinta knowing no English and very little French. I drank the entire pot of tea, as it was excellent as Alice had claimed. I also ate most of the cookies, obviously not homemade, thinking regretfully that I was a few years too late to have the pleasure of sampling Alice's famous brownies.

The talk turned naturally to books, especially Stein's books, which by this time were beginning to be in demand again. I remarked how much I had had to pay for a copy of *Lucy Church Amiably*, the first title published by Alice in her capacity as the publisher of the now famous Plain Edition series which she and Gertrude had launched during the bleak years when Stein despaired of ever being commercially published. A Picasso had been sold to finance this endeavor, and eventually five titles were published. At least one more in the series was planned, but then along came *The Autobiography*

Last known photo of Alice B. Toklas (by Robert Wilson)

of Alice B. Toklas together with fame and success and no more problems in getting published.

Alice was astonished at the price I had paid and said that she had a couple of cartons of them still around, which I promptly offered to buy, having by this time become the owner of the Phoenix. Correspondence about the method of shipment of them ensued all that summer, but no books ever appeared. Apparently Alice had been mistaken.

By this time I had stayed about forty-five minutes and rose to go, not wanting to tire her too much. Alice immediately said, "Oh, don't go if you don't have to."

I replied, "But I was told when I was brought up that no one ever stayed more than half an hour on a first visit."

"Well, I'm from the West. We're not so delicate. Sit down," she replied.

That being a royal command, I sat back down, glad to prolong the visit. Her brilliant and sparkling conversation continued despite her age and infirmity. As the minutes passed, I continued to marvel that at the age of eighty-seven, in failing health, she was so vibrant and compelling a personality. I could only wonder what she must have been like in her prime.

Eventually I felt courageous enough to bring up the subject of the paintings, saying how sorry I was that they were gone. Alice sighed resignedly, saying, "Well, by now my memory of them is better than my eyesight." And then she straightened up in her chair, adding, "It's all the fault of that Armenian woman," referring of course to the widow of Allen Stein. Then, realizing that perhaps she had made a betise, she looked straight at me, her beautiful baritone voice descending almost to a basso profundo, added, "I'm not being unkind. It's not my fault if there's a stigma attached to being Armenian."

By now I had stayed three hours. She bade me adieu and I left, making a detour through the dining room to have a look at the high-backed Spanish chairs so familiar from the early photos taken of the Stein studio at the rue de Fleurus.

This was destined to be my last visit with her. We continued to correspond through Alice's amanuensis, since cataracts had left her eyesight too poor for reading or writing. In 1967, just as I was on the verge on leaving for Paris to see her again, she died and was buried in Père Lachaise Cemetery in Paris, together with her beloved Gertrude.

Glenway, D.J., and the Tigers

For many years I had known of Glenway Wescott as an author whose books were still in some slight demand among collectors and institutional libraries. I had seen him at the annual convocations of the American Academy of Arts and Letters; I was also familiar with the name of Monroe Wheeler as the publisher of the "Manikin" pamphlets, highly treasured early titles by Marianne Moore, William Carlos Williams, and Glenway himself. Then one day in the 1970s Glenway appeared in person in the shop along with Wheeler. After some incidental conversation, Monroe revealed the purpose of their visit. To my surprise and delight they offered me multiple copies—mint and unopened—of the beautifully designed and printed "Harrison of Paris" series of books, published in Paris in the early '30s.

The timing of issuing these was disastrous for them—the very depths of the Great Depression. Despite the sumptuous formats of these editions of well-established authors illustrated by top rank artists, very few copies were sold. The books had, therefore, been difficult to find now that there was an increasing demand for them, especially two early titles by Katherine Anne Porter—*Hacienda* and *French Song,* and *The Fables of Aeso*p illustrated by Alexander Calder. Other rarities included a signed extremely limited edition of a portion of Thomas Mann's autobiography, Glenway's *A Calendar of Saints for Unbelievers* illustrated by Pavel Tchelitchev, and Byron's *Childe Harold's Pilgrimage* illustrated by Sir Francis Rose, Gertrude Steins last pro-

Glenway Wescott

tégé in the art world. Not only had Glenway and Monroe brought me pristine copies, they also assured me that I would be allowed more copies whenever I needed them. This worked well for everyone concerned, and gradually I came to know the two men better and better.

Monroe Wheeler

Eventually I felt enough at ease to ask if they would ever consider selling books out of their personal library, believing that there would be a great many treasures. They had, after all, lived in Paris during the height of the expatriate period and had obviously known many of the renowned writers of the time. The answer was an immediate, "Yes, we'll do that sometime."

I was delighted when, not long after that, I was invited to spend a weekend at their home in southern New Jersey outside a small town called Rosemont, located on the Pennsylvania border near Lambertville. Amazingly, I found my way there by car with very little difficulty, and was immediately charmed by the eighteenth-century fieldstone house in which they lived. After lunch I was shown the major part of the library in the living room, which was dominated by a huge walk-in fireplace. Additionally there were books all over the house, but this was the only area in which I would be allowed to make selections.

I was dazzled, and wanted, of course, almost everything. Bur Monroe didn't want to part with very many books at one time, which I could readily understand. Since he was not in need of money, it was difficult to persuade him to part with many of my choices. What would become a routine over the years was for me to make my selections, pull the books out from the shelves, and pencil my offers onto the fly-leaves. Then while I chatted with Glenway, Monroe would go through the choices, and invariably replace most of my choices on his shelves. Generally I came away with about ten percent of what I wanted. But over the years, with patience and many repeated visits, I managed to obtain almost all of my original choices. The final disposition of the remaining ten percent is an unhappy tale which has no place in this memoir.

After this had been completed, Glenway announced that we were expected at his brother's house for dinner. I learned at this point that his brother Lloyd had married Barbara Harrison, who had founded the book publishing venture which bore her name, "Harrison of Paris. "She supplied the money, Glenway selected and edited the texts, and Monroe designed the books. On her return to the United States she had settled in Stone Blossom in a picturesque New Jersey valley, but this property had to be abandoned when a dam was built nearby, flooding the entire valley. She then purchased a large four hundred acre farm known as "Hay Meadow", on which were three large houses. She and Lloyd lived in one, their daughter Deborah in another with her husband Thane, and Glenway and Monroe in the third (and oldest) one. So we all got into Monroe's car and drove

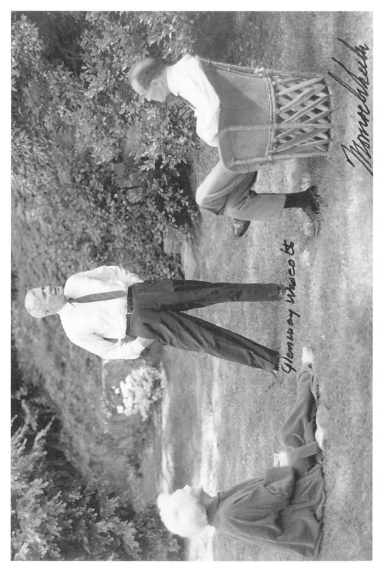

Katherine Ann Porter, Glenway Wescott, and Monroe Wheeler, Washington, DC, 1965

about a quarter of a mile to Lloyd's house. I learned than that Barbara had died a few months earlier.

The four of us were seated around the dining room table, where I felt as though I was dining in a small gallery of a major museum. Opposite me was a large Utrillo, and behind me were a Renoir and a Cezanne. Glenway told me later that "the really good things" had been sold off after Barbara's death in order to settle her estate. I could only wonder what they might have been if these were the leftovers! We were being served by a person wearing a white shirt and blue jeans, with a very low, androgynous voice. I could not make up my mind as to the gender. but my puzzlement was soon forgotten when Lloyd remarked, "Debbo's kittens are getting very large."

Cat lover that I am, I immediately asked, "What kind of kittens?", expecting to hear Siamese or Burmese, or one of the other popular show breeds.

"Oh, she's got two tiger cubs," came the reply that almost caused me to choke.

"Where?"

"Down at her house."

"Can we go see them?" I asked in high excitement.

"Your dessert will be spoiled," Lloyd replied.

"Oh, please; I can eat dessert any time."

"Well, it's getting dark and they may have gone to bed by this time." But seeing the look of disappointment on my face, he continued, "I'll try." He left the table, telephoned, and returned, saying, "It will be okay if we go right away."

I dropped my spoon immediately, abandoning my ice cream, and jumped up, the others following at a slightly more dignified pace. Getting into Lloyd's car, we drove a couple of miles in almost total darkness, He turned into an unmarked driveway, flanked on either side by high grass, and stopped the car. I scrambled out, and almost at once had one of the greatest thrills of my entire life, for there, coming through the grass, were two large tiger cubs, their eyes blazing fiery green in the car's headlights. It was not a forest, but it was night and those tigers were indisputably "burning bright." Later I wondered how Blake could have realized the intensity of the light reflected from tigers' eyes. Certainly he never met a tiger head-on in this fashion?

Introductions were made to Lloyd's daughter and son-in-law. I wanted of course to touch the "kittens", but didn't know if it was safe or permitted. So I asked and was told that I could, but warned that they were still cubs and could get unintentionally rough. If they started chewing too hard or got too rambunctious I was told to put my fingers into their mouths and pull back at the corners and they would cease. A risky business, I thought, putting your hand into a tiger's mouth, even if it is only a "kitten". Months later, on return visits, I did this—and more- quite often. But now, nothing daunted, I started petting and playing with them. and in true cat fashion, they rolled over to have their bellies rubbed, and eventually one of them grabbed hold with its front claws and started kicking with its hind feet, exactly as all my own cats were wont to do. So I did as instructed and found that it worked. After about fifteen minutes of this Debbo and her husband announced that the cubs were up past their bedtime; they had stayed up longer than usual just so I could see them, but must now be put to bed.

So we left and went back to Glenway's house. On the way back I found out why the tiger cubs were there. Tiger mothers will not raise their offspring in captivity, and destroy any such cubs. So cubs that are born in zoos are removed from their mothers at birth and hand-raised by specialists. These two were Siberians, of which fewer than two hundred specimens were known to be extant, so that it was all the more imperative to raise them to maturity. They were females named Nina and Shura, in honor of two great Russian ballerinas. Even though we went to bed shortly after eleven p.m. that night, my adrenaline was so high it was almost dawn before I fell asleep.

When I returned home the following day, my roommate Kenneth was madly jealous, and nothing would do but that I arrange for another visit so he too could experience the tigers. Glenway and Monroe were agreeable, and volunteered to ask Debbo and Thane if they and the tigers were in a mood for another visit. It was arranged, and in fact, turned out even better than we had hoped, for Lloyd had to be away from home for a few days, and had asked his daughter to baby-sit the art treasures in his home while he was away. This meant bringing the tiger cubs with her. and as it was summer, we were told to bring swim gear for the pool on the estate.

To our surprise we learned that tigers, unlike almost all other cats, were fond of water, and enjoyed swimming in the pool. We had to be careful, though, to see that they did not get too tired, and also to help them get out of the pool, since they could not get a grip on the tiles on the edging. This time I had my camera with me, resulting in a wonderful series of pictures of us holding the tigers in our arms, sitting on the edge of the pool, and most dazzling to all our friends back in New York, our hands in the tigers' mouths. Further visits ensued, with more photos as the tigers grew larger. Then there was a gap of over a year.

Eventually Monroe and Glenway asked if I wanted to come down and select some more books. Off I went on a Saturday. After the book dealing concluded on Sunday morning, I inquired about the tigers, and found they were now so large, having reached their full growth of nearly seven hundred pounds, that they were living in a large pen enclosing slightly over two acres, with a stone house in it for shelter. It was so well-appointed that Glenway remarked that it was like a concentration camp for Rothschilds.

Glenway asked if I wanted to visit them, and of course I said that I did. We went over to the cage and Thane asked if I wanted to go in with Nina. It turned out that Nina was in the cage alone, as her sister Shura was not so even-tempered, and they had to be kept apart. Nina was reliable and very friendly; Shura could be aggressive, and a seven hundred pound

Robert Wilson holding Nina and
Kenneth Doubrava holding Shura

aggressive tigress is something not to be casual about. I wasn't too sure about going in with Nina, friendly or not, even though she was not supposed to be aggressive. I asked if she had had her breakfast before I decided to risk it.

Thane told me to go up to the cage and call her. She came over to the fence immediately, and then Thane told me to stand close to it so she could sniff my scent. Apparently tigers have excellent memories and can remember the distinctive personal scent of any animal they have previously encountered—including humans. So Nina sniffed a couple of times, and apparently remembered me, for she thereupon rolled over on her back wanting me to scratch her belly. So I gladly went in and did just that, although I must admit doing so with the precaution of a stick, for a serious mauling could ensue just out of playfulness. Once again, more photos, including the one that is my favorite to this day, with Nina stretched out regally in the "Library Lion" pose, with me just a bit behind her head, my hand on top of it.

I later learned that Nina had become a TV celebrity by being the first tiger to be used in the famous Exxon commercials. She was earning her and her sister's keep, very helpful since they consumed forty pounds of horse meat per day. I can recognize the commercials with Nina in them as opposed to later ones with her successor, for the striped markings on a tiger's face are all different, resembling Chinese characters, and once you learn to recognize them you can always tell whether it is your friend or a stranger. Very useful information when you encounter tigers in your daily rounds.

The next morning Monroe asked me to drive him back to New York, and since I felt that I had known him and Glenway long enough by this time, I took this opportunity to ask him a couple of somewhat personal questions that had been in the back of my mind for some time.

It was perfectly obvious to everyone who knew them that there was constant bickering between them, but never any fights. They usually had a housekeeper who prepared their meals, but on days when she was not present Glenway habitually prepared the meals. Monroe invariably complained about some feature of the meal, and conversely Glenway was always complaining about what he perceived as Monroe's forgetfulness. The bickering went on almost incessantly, but neither one of them deigned to answer the other. Obviously they had lived together long enough that this had become a familiar litany that need not be acknowledged. So I asked Monroe how long they had been together.

Robert Wilson with the full-grown 700 pound Nina

He replied that it had been sixty-three years. "I think we ought to be in *The Guinness Book of Records* for the longest enduing gay alliance in history," he replied with a chuckle. "And they say gay liaisons don't last!"

I then asked how they had gotten together, and Monroe went on to explain that he was living in Chicago at the time, and one cold winter day he was walking down the street and saw lying inert on the sidewalk, either unconscious or dead, the most beautiful teen-age boy he had ever seen. He stopped and investigated and found the boy had fainted, so he picked him up and literally carried him home. Upon being revived, the young man told his story. He had left Wisconsin and had come to Chicago to get away from family pressures because of his homosexuality, but had been unable to find employment, had been evicted from his rooming house, and had actually fainted from lack of food. Thus began the relationship which had endured all those years, into a seventh decade. Luckily for Glenway, Monroe had sufficient funds to keep them both until Glenway's novels began bringing in enough money for him to have his own income, at least enough not to have the stigma of being "kept."

Having broken the ice on questions, I decided I could now ask about the androgynous creature who had been our servitor the night of the first encounter with the tigers. I confessed that I had been totally unable to determine the gender.

"Oh, that was D.J., Monroe replied.

This helped me not at all. "D.J.?" I repeated.

"Yes, D.J. She is one of the trustees from the state penitentiary. Barbara and Lloyd always thought it their duty to help rehabilitate prisoners. Both D.J. and the cook are allowed out if they can find work. I've often told Lloyd the we are going to wake up and find ourselves murdered in our beds. But he insists that we are safer than anyone else in the county. No one would dare break in knowing that those two (meaning D.J. and the cook whom I hadn't seen) were on the premises."

My curiosity was definitely piqued by now. "What were they in for?"

In his usual, deadpan throwaway manner Monroe answered with a single word: "Murder!"

Upon further prodding, Monroe elaborated. The one who had served us was the daughter of a local policeman, and she had been having a Lesbian love affair, a fact that was common knowledge in the small town where she lived. One day, as she boarded the local bus, the driver made a smart-aleck crack about her lover. D.J got off the bus at once, went home and got one of her father's pistols and waited for the same bus to come back on its return route. When it appeared, she got on again and calmly shot the driver at point-blank range. As there were witnesses, and it was obviously premeditated, there was only one possible verdict at the trial. Since New Jersey did not have the death penalty, she was given a long sentence. By the time I encountered her she had served most of it, and was now a "trustee", along with the girlfriend, who had been convicted as an accomplice.

By now we were driving through the Lincoln Tunnel into Manhattan. What an eventful weekend that visit had been. And what a haul I had made away with—a first edition of T.S. Eliot's *The Waste Land,* two tigresses, and a pair of murderesses!

Louis Zukovsky

My first encounter with Louis Zukovsky was a rather querulous phone call from him asking why I was selling some of his private correspondence. I was both startled and amused, since what he was referring to was an innocuous postcard he had sent to someone arranging a meeting, which I had acquired as part of a small collection of literary autographs. I explained to him exactly what it was, and that terminated the call. I had, of course, known who he was. I also knew that in the world of poetry he was held in high esteem by two of the giants, Ezra Pound and William Carlos Williams, and also by several of the younger generation, including many whom I knew personally, especially Robert Duncan and Robert Creeley.

Six weeks after this initial contact, I received another telephone call from him, this time asking if I could come to Brooklyn to buy a lot of books. He and his wife Celia were moving to Manhattan and wanted to divest themselves of a large part of their library. I agreed immediately, imagining all sorts of treasures that I might acquire.

Once there though, I was dismayed at what was shown me. It was six large cartons, mainly heavily used textbooks that were no longer of use to him now that he was retired from teaching. There were half a dozen copies of the original edition of his *A Test of Poetry*, a title that was very scarce and in rather considerable demand. But they were so heavily worn that the bindings were falling off the pages. Nonetheless I bought the lot, and hoped for better things later on.

There was one positive aspect about this transaction. Apparently I had made a good enough impression on Louis and Celia for them to make me a gift of an unopened copy of one of his privately published books,

Barely and Widely, which became the initial item in my own personal collection of his works.

After they moved to Manhattan, to a rather elegant apartment on Fifty-ninth Street overlooking Central Park, I was invited about once a year to come buy more books. These were usually review books, and once in a while, some really desirable books that had been sent them by some of their younger admirers, particularly Duncan and Creeley. Occasionally there would be extra copies of the latest book by Louis himself, carefully identified in his minute handwriting as "Desk Copy" or "Extra Copy."

Knowing full well that his sales were not large, and the consequent royalties must have been minuscule to say the least, I often wondered how they afforded such an obviously high-priced apartment. From other sources I learned that a wealthy admirer was subsidizing the rent. Apparently at some point this patron had to cut back, for after a few years they moved to an apartment in a building owned by the same chain as the Central Park one, but now on the border of Greenwich Village, just north of Fourteenth Street. The apartment was almost identical, but without a view. This change of residence meant that I saw them more often, for it was within easy walking distance of the Phoenix. Quite often in good weather Louis and Celia would come out for a stroll after dinner and stop in for a chat.

They were a strange couple in many ways; both were tiny, thin almost to emaciation, and both virtual chain-smokers. In fact, one of the poets who knew them well told me semi-jokingly that he believed they lived solely off cigarettes and coffee. Louis' eyesight was very poor; the lenses in his glasses were as thick as the proverbial Coke-bottle bottoms. Of the four different residences in which I visited them, sparseness was the keynote. Everything—furniture, books, decorations—was held to the absolute minimum. I once thought they would have been totally at home in a Shaker community.

I'm always interested in examining people's libraries, especially those of poets. Book accumulations always reveal a great deal about the owner's interests. The Zukovsky library, like it's owner, was tiny: his own books of course, a few by Pound and Williams, (presentation copies, it might be noted) and then the complete Loeb classical library. And nothing else whatever. Louis' great passion was the entire corpus of Greek and Latin literature, an interest which was shared by his wife, whose métier was reputedly composing music.

Unfortunately, I'm afraid that her work had little to recommend it. Other than their only child Paul, who was a concert violinist, no one seemed willing to give it a public performance—with one notable exception.

David Stivender, the chorus master of the Metropolitan Opera, who was single-handedly responsible for turning that group from a mediocre one into one of the best in the world, had become a regular visitor to the Phoenix. He was very much interested in modern literature, had come across some poems by Zukovsky, and had arrived at the Phoenix in his search for some of the scarce volumes. Not long after his initial visit, I asked David if he would like to meet Zukovsky. He was thrilled at the prospect and I arranged an introduction. They got on well together, and eventually David conceived the idea of arranging for a performance of a long poem by Louis entitled *Autobiography* which had been published in book form with Celia's musical setting of the entire text. David got four of his principal choristers to attempt the piece at the Metropolitan Opera Studio. To David's dismay, the musical setting proved simply impossible to perform. So David had to rewrite it himself. Whether Celia realized what he had done or not, the eventual performance was a success.

When the University of Texas wanted to acquire Louis' entire archive, he would agree only if they would publish his large work *Bottom: On Shakespeare,* a massive work which had also been set to music by Celia. Texas agreed, and duly issued it in two thick quarto volumes as a boxed set, one volume containing the text and the other the musical setting.. Sales were pitifully small, and some years later the edition was remaindered. And to the best of my knowledge there has never been a performance.

Louis and Celia seemed to like me, and once when they were visiting the shop during the summer, I asked Louis to write something in my guest book. He agreed and wrote out the text of a new poem which he had called *Finally a Valentine.* At the end of it he wrote "Homage to Bob and his tan", referring to the deep tan I had acquired spending much time on the beach at Fire Island. The following February this poem appeared as a Valentine's Day card in England. Of course I laid a copy into the guest book. But its next appearance truly astounded me. Some time after the assassination of President Kennedy, an anthology of poems called *Of Power and Poetry* appeared, being announced as poems composed in honor of the late president. And there was *Finally a Valentine* with the title dropped! I could only shake my head in amazement at how much mileage Louis could get out of a single poem.

After a couple of years in the Greenwich Village apartment, the Zukovskys moved to Port Jefferson on Long Island, near one of the state universities. It so happened that one day I had an appointment with Louis Simpson, the Pulitzer Prize winner who was teaching there' so I decided that as long as I was nearby, I would take a chance of finding the Zukovskys at home and pay an impromptu visit. I knew that they did not own a car, nor could even of them drive, so the chances were good of finding them at home. They were indeed, and invited me in, but asked me if I minded waiting a bit as they were working on his translation of Catullus, something that had been in progress for several years. As I sat and listened, I could make no sense of what was going on. But slowly it began to come clear. Celia and Louis were pacing about the room, cigarettes in hand, speaking the Latin out loud, line for line, and then trying to find English words that had roughly the same sound. When a lucky hit was made, it was committed to paper for Louis to work into the ongoing translation. Some years later it was published, but reviewers and scholars alike found the text of Louis' purported translation to be the same as my assessment: a noble effort, but no more comprehensible than the original Latin.

Due to the distance from New York City, that visit turned out to by my last, for Louis died only a little over a year later, in May 1979, and Celia died about a year after Louis. Despite the support and encouragement from Ezra Pound and William Carlos Williams, both of whom regarded Louis as a peer, the general public never took to his work. However many of the succeeding generation of poets, especially the Black Mountain group, found much in his work rewarding, and an inspiration for their own efforts. This lack of public acclaim obviously did not deter Louis. He was the most dedicated of craftsmen; I never heard a complaint, and he labored endlessly to keep at his work. He devoted virtually every waking minute of his life to the perfection of his poems. His holograph manuscripts are amazing to behold. Every line, every word was worked and reworked, endlessly it seems.

I once saw some pages from his long, ongoing poem *A*. It was so massively rewritten that I doubt anyone could follow the progression of the revisions. There was virtually no white space left visible. It was as densely packed as were the work sheets of Joyce and Proust, probably the two most assiduous revisers in modern literary history. Louis gave up everything for his work. I can only hope that his dedication will ultimately be recognized more widely.

Seeing Shelley Plain

Part Three

The Players:
Writers Discussed in the Memoirs

It was suggested by one reader while this book was still "a work in progress" that I should make some identification of the various poets who appear in these memoirs. He felt that while those readers who are passionately interested in modern American poetry might be familiar with most if not all of them, to many others they are not "household names". I therefore offer these résumés in order to better acquaint readers with the various characters herein discussed.

Helen Adam
1909–1993

Helen Adam was a charming, elfin Scots poet. She was a child prodigy and had three substantial volumes of poetry published in England in the 1920s. Her first book *The Elfin Peddler* appeared to great acclaim in 1923. After World War II she emigrated to the United States, settling in San Francisco where she became part of the then emerging younger generation of poets. She was particularly close to Robert Duncan. Later she moved to New York, where she lived until her death.

John Ashbery
1927–

Along with Frank O'Hara, Kenneth Koch, and James Schuyler, Ashbery is one of the leaders of the group that became known as "The New York School." Following a privately published pamphlet, *Turandot*, his first published book *Some Trees* appeared in 1956 in the distinguished Yale Younger Poet series. He subsequently went on to win all three major prizes, the Pulitzer, the Bollingen, and the National Book Award. for his volume *Self Portrait in a Convex Mirror*.

W.H. Auden
1907–1973

Wystan Hugh Auden was born in York, England, the youngest of three sons of George Augustus and Constance Bicknell Auden. At Oxford he met Christopher Isherwood, two years his senior, and they formed a life-long friendship. Auden had intended to be a mining engineer, but started writing poetry, and eventually announced to his tutor his decision to change his area of study. The tutor, not unexpectedly, was highly skeptical, and questioned the wisdom and practicality of such a move. Auden's reply was, "But sir, I shall be a great poet."

The tutor's reply has not been recorded, but, against all likelihood, Auden made good on this declaration, becoming one of the greatest poets writing in English in this century. In fact, the critical evaluation puts him in a direct line of descent from Yeats to Pound to Eliot to Auden. It is also interesting to note that in this hierarchy, each one was instrumental in getting his successor published.

Auden's first book was a small pamphlet, hand printed on a miniature press by his friend Stephen Spender in 1928 (who also printed his own first book in a similar manner.) Actual publication came two years later when Faber & Faber, whose poetry editor was T.S. Eliot, published Auden's *Poems*. This was followed by *The Orators*, which received considerable favorable acclaim. Following this there were three plays written in collaboration with Isherwood in the late 1930s. By 1938 both Isherwood and Auden were unhappy with the atmosphere in England, and emigrated to the United

States. Auden took up permanent residence (and ultimately became a U.S. citizen,) while Isherwood settled in California. Auden received many literary awards, including the Pulitzer Prize in 1948 for *The Age of Anxiety.* In 1970 he decided to return to England and became the Poet in Residence at Oxford, where he spent the academic season. While residing in his permanent home in Kirchstettin, Austria, a tiny village not far from Vienna, he died in his sleep in 1973.

Ted Berrigan
1934–1983

Although he was generally regarded as the leading light of the "Second Generation" of the so-called New York School, most of Berrigan's work was published either in mimeographed form or by small press publishers. He never achieved a following large enough to attract a mainstream publisher, and lived in the East Village until his death.

Elizabeth Bishop
1911–1979

Born in Nova Scotia, Bishop was raised by her American grandparents. She attended Vassar, and is widely believed to be the model for one of the characters in Mary McCarthy's *The Group.* Her first book, *North and South,* appeared to great acclaim in 1946. Her second volume, *Poems—North and South and a Cold Spring* appeared in 1955 and won the Pulitzer Prize. She lived in Brazil from 1951 until the death of her companion Lota de Marchado Soares in 1966, at which time she returned to the U.S where she died suddenly in 1979.

The Black Mountain School

Founded by Charles Olson in a remote part of North Carolina in 1948, this school lasted only three years. In order to publicize the school and in the hope of attracting students, Olson launched a magazine entitled, appropriately, *The Black Mountain Review* under the editorship of Robert Creeley. Unfortunately the cost of producing the magazine ate up all the available funds, and the school was forced to close. It had been devoted to the humanities, with a multidiscipline curriculum. It attracted poets John Wieners and Joel Oppenheimer, fiction writer Fielding Dawson, artist Cy Twombly, and printer-publisher Jonathan Williams, whose Jargon Press published many of the early works of the members of this school.

Robert Bly
1926–

Bly's career has been spent mainly in the upper Midwest. In the 1970s he was one of the founders of the Ox Head Press. His circle includes Donald Hall and W.D. Snodgrass. His novel *Iron John* had phenomenal success late in his career.

Louise Bogan
1897–1970

Born in Livermore Falls, Maine, Bogan never received the recognition which was her due. Her output was small, since by choice she never published anything but her very best work. For more than twenty years she was poetry critic for the *New Yorker* and was also Consultant in Poetry at the Library of Congress in 1945-46. (This title has been changed to Poet Laureate.) In 1954 her *Collected Poems* won the Bollingen Prize.

William S. Burroughs
1914–1997

Among the Beats, Burroughs is one of the major figures whose influence seems to be growing. He worked solely in the field of fiction, and had his second novel, *Naked Lunch,* published in Paris in 1959 by the then notorious Traveler's Companion series. In it, he introduced the "cut-up" method, now recognized as a radical change in the art of fiction.

Ann Charters

Beginning with her bibliography of Kerouac in 1967, followed short-ly by the first biography of him, and then a critical work on Charles Olson, Charters has established herself as an authority on the Beats. She has also edited several anthologies in this field.

Gregory Corso
1930–

In a blurb on Corso's second book, *Gasoline,* Allen Ginsberg described him as "the one true poet of us all." A native New Yorker, Corso lived in Paris in the late '50s at the famous "Beat Hotel' along with Ginsberg, Burroughs, Alan Ansen and other Beats. *Gasoline,* which contains his best work, was published by City Lights in 1958 in its landmark Pocket Poets series. One of his most famous poems is *Bomb,* dealing with the atomic bomb, and printed in broadside format in the shape of a mushroom cloud.

Robert Creeley
1926–

Along with Duncan, Levertov and Wieners, Robert Creeley is one of the major members of the group around Charles Olson known as the "Black Mountain" poets. His first book *Le Fou* appeared in 1952, and his poetic output has been voluminous. He lived abroad for many years, but for the past two decades has taught at the State University at Buffalo.

Diane di Prima
1930–

Born in New York, di Prima is by all odds the leading female poet of the Beat generation and the acknowledged peer of the male members of the group. Her talents are diverse and her energy prodigious, managing a little theater, co-editing a newspaper with LeRoi Jones (later to become Amiri Baraka,) translating novels and poetry, and raising five children, all the while producing her own poetry. She currently resides on the West Coast, where she continues to write poetry while teaching and writing her memoirs.

Robert Duncan
1919-1988

Duncan is generally considered one of the major poets of the "Black Mountain" group. His entire poetic career was based in San Francisco. He was closely associated with Robert Creeley and Denise Levertov, and for many years his work appeared solely from little presses, although many were substantial enough to produce superbly printed volumes. In the last two decades of his career his reputation had grown enough for him to be published by New Directions, certainly one of the major publishers in the post-war decades.

Isabella Gardner
1915-1981

Gardner was what is generally spoken of as a "minor poet". She received polite reviews, but never achieved status equal to that of her contemporaries. Her output was relatively small—three volumes.

Jean Garrigue
1913-1972

Although she was often unjustly considered a minor poet, Garrigue's six volumes show virtuosity and mastery of form coupled with trenchant observation. It remains a mystery why this superb poet never received widespread acclaim although she was regarded as a peer by such distinguished poets as Stanley Kunitz, Richard Eberhard, and May Swenson, among many others.

H. Rider Haggard
1856–1925

Haggard was an extremely prolific Victorian novelist, most of whose work was set in South Africa. He is primarily remembered for his novels *King Solomon's Mines* and *She*.

Donald Hall
1928–

Donald Hall has had a distinguished career as a poet, and has also authored several well-received children's books and many works of criticism. Additionally he has edited numerous excellent anthologies. He lives on the farm in New Hampshire where he spent his childhood with his grandparents.

Barbara Howes
1914–1996

Howes was born in Boston, and for many years was married to the poet William Jay Smith, with whom she had two sons. After some years in Europe following World War II, they returned to the U.S. and lived in North Pownal, Vermont. An accomplished poet and anthologist, she unfortunately never received the critical acclaim many think was her due.

LeRoi Jones
1934–

Born in Newark, New Jersey, Jones burst on the poetic scene in 1961 with his first volume of poetry *Preface to a Twenty Volume Suicide Note* (preceded only by a small political tract about Cuba). He immediately became the editor of *Yugen,* a seminal magazine running for seven issues in the early '60s. Hard on the heels of this he co-edited with Diane di Prima the very important *The Floating Bear.* Toward the end of the '60s he began writing plays and created considerable sensation with *Dutchman.* At the time of

Malcolm X's assassination he became a militant Black activist and changed his name to Amiri Baraka, which he has retained to this day.

Denise Levertov
1923–1997

This Welsh-born poet came to America as a war bride in 1946, having married Mitchell Goodman. They lived briefly in Guatemala, but then settled in New York City. Her first book *The Double Image* was published in England. After that she got a big boost when her second book *Here and Now* appeared in the distinguished City Lights Pocket Poet series. She soon got in touch with Robert Duncan and Robert Creeley, and is generally regarded as one of the major poets in the group known as "The Black Mountain School," although none of the three actually was in residence at the famous school run by Charles Olson.

Michael McClure
1932–

McClure is perhaps the most interesting of all the Beats because he has consistently dared more, pushing the boundaries further than any other poet that I know of still writing. His first book *Passage* appeared in 1956. McClure is equally prolific in the field of drama, and it is here that he continues to experiment with both form and content. His play *Josephine the Mouse Singer* won an Obie in 1979. His earlier play *The Beard* created a sensation when it was first performed in San Francisco, attracting the attention of the police because of the performance of oral sex during the play. The actors were arrested every night, and the arrest rapidly became a highlight of the performance, at least for most of the audience. While it was never produced on Broadway, the distinguished editor, book collector and critic William Targ declared that he ranked it along with Beckett's *Waiting for Godot* as one of the two most important plays of the second half of the 20th century.

Eve Merriam
1916-1995

Merriam is another poet whose true worth has never been recognized. Her poetic career began with the publication of her first book *Family Circle* in the distinguished Yale Younger Poets series. a prolific writer, she issued several volumes of trenchant, witty verse, dozens of very successful children's books, biographies, criticism and successful plays.

James Merrill
1926-1995

At first regarded as a wealthy dilettante, Merrill very quickly was given due recognition as one of the most richly endowed poets of his generation. Two privately produced books preceded his first actual publication, a volume entitled *First Poems* which appeared in 1951. He went on to win universal admiration for the multilayered brilliance of his work. The first volume in what became his *magnum opus* was entitled *Divine Comedies,* appearing in 1976. Two further volumes appeared, and then the complete work was published under the title *The Changing Light at Sandover.* Merrill claimed that the work was dictated by a spirit which he and his partner reached through a Ouija board. This brought on some derision, but whether or not it was true there is no denying the enormous brilliance of the work. Merrill went on to win the National Book Award twice, as well as capturing the Bollingen Prize and the Pulitzer.

Marianne Moore
1887-1972

Moore is, of course, one of the giants of 20th-century American poetry. Her first commercially published book *Observations* appeared in 1924, preceded by two small privately published pamphlets. Her poetry is unlike that of any other major poet, being based on syllabics rather than metrics. Her *Collected Poems* won the Pulitzer Prize in 1950. Shortly thereafter she embarked on a major enterprise which occupied her time for many years, namely translating the *Fables* of La Fontaine. This enormous work finally appeared in 1954. A great baseball fan, she was once invited to throw out the opening ball of the season, an honor usually reserved for Presidents of the United States. She was almost as well known for her eccentric garb as for her poetry, generally appearing in public in a voluminous cape with a Colonial era tricorn hat perched atop her once-red hair.

Nanda Pivano

Not a poet herself, Pivano is one of the most important figures of American literature due to her courageous espousal of American writing at a time when it was dangerous to do so, and for her postwar generous subsidizing of American poets by getting them published and widely known in Europe, especially in Italy.

Ezra Pound
1885-1972

By all odds the most controversial poet of the 20th century, Pound is also the most influential. Pound left the U.S. in 1907, returning once in the late 1930s in an attempt to talk to government officials about the impending war. From the very beginning he immersed himself in poetry, and prior to World War I became William Butler Yeats' secretary. Many feel that Pound's influence helped spur the great burst of Yeats' late work. He was tireless in his promotion of the works of others, and almost single-handedly launched the career of T.S. Eliot by editing an anthology—*The Catholic Anthology*—in which Eliot made his first appearance in print with his famous "Prufrock". Later, as is now well known, he heavily edited and corrected *The Waste Land*. After the war Pound moved to Paris briefly, and finally settled in Rapallo, Italy. When the U.S. entered the Second World War Pound tried to bring his family back to the U.S., but an idiotic American consul refused to allow Pound's natural daughter (by his mistress Olga Rudge) to accompany the family. Since it was unthinkable to leave a teen-age daughter alone without funds in the middle of a war, the Pounds all elected to stay in Italy. It was then that Pound made the drastic mistake of delivering a long series of broadcasts over the Italian radio. When the war was over, Pound was immediately arrested on a charge of treason, and was kept in an open-air cage for several weeks in the broiling Italian sun in a prison camp near Pisa. Eventually he was brought to Washington, but the case never came to trial, and Pound was incarcerated in an insane asylum in Washington D.C for twelve years. The content of the radio broadcasts could not be proven treasonable, and eventually public opinion shifted and Pound was released, going back to Italy and living his remaining days with Olga Rudge in Venice. He continued to work on his long, ongoing *Cantos* right up until his death in 1972. While in the asylum he became the center of an enormous literary controversy when his *Pisan Cantos* won the prestigious Bollingen Prize in 1949. At the time, critical opinion was heavily weighted against Pound due to the unproved treason charges and his regrettable use of anti-Semitic language. Nowadays these two factors are mostly overlooked in the light of his obvious literary importance.

Tim Reynolds

In the beginning of the Beat period, Reynolds, although not a Beat poet, was considered to be potentially an important poet, and had the encouragement of Ezra Pound. But for some unknown reason, he simply stopped writing and disappeared from the scene.

Laura Riding
1901-1991

Laura Riding, born Laura Reichenthal, was for most of her life her own worst enemy. An extreme perfectionist in her own work, she demanded the same standards of everyone with whom she came in contact, and often alienated readers and critics otherwise inclined to be favorable. After separating from a disastrous early marriage, she went to Europe and entered into a long-running liaison with Robert Graves. When this ended dramatically with a failed suicide that left her permanently crippled, she returned to the U.S. and married Schuyler Jackson. Ever after she insisted on being known as Laura (Riding) Jackson, and abandoned poetry, totally devoting herself to criticism and work on a dictionary which was never completed. She died in Wabasso, Florida in 1991.

Ed Sanders

One of the most colorful of the Beats, Sanders has continued writing poetry, but undoubtedly will be remembered for his ground-breaking magazine, *FUCK YOU/ a magazine of the arts.* Its name in no way described the content. It contained nothing even vaguely pornographic or even objectionable. It was merely an attention-getting device, and contained the latest work by the major Beat poets. It was so successful that Ed extended it well beyond his announced intention to stop after six issues. Finally the police arrested him and impounded all the copies he had in his bookshop. Several well known literary figures joined the defense, the magazine was declared not pornographic, and Sanders was released. But somehow, the police "could not find" any of the several hundred copies of the magazine that they had impounded. In addition to poetry he has published fiction and a documentary study of Charles Manson entitled *The Family.*

Delmore Schwartz
1913–1966

Schwartz' first volume *In Dreams Begin Responsibilities* was greeted with rhapsodic reviews. Unfortunately his subsequent work did not live up to this promise, and by the time of his death in 1966 in a seedy 42nd Street hotel, he was almost totally forgotten.

Karl Shapiro
1913–

Born in Baltimore, Shapiro attracted considerable attention for his second (and first published) book, *Person, Place and Thing,* but unfortunately his later work never role to the level of that early work. He has had, nonetheless, a distinguished career, being the Consultant in Poetry at the Library of Congress, and was also editor for several years of the granddaddy of all American Poetry magazines, the Chicago-based *Poetry.*

Gary Snyder
1930–

A West Coast poet, Snyder studied for several years at a Buddhist monastery in Kyoto, publishing his first book of poetry there. Upon his return to the U.S. he settled in California. He won the Pulitzer prize in 1974 for *Turtle Island.*

Dylan Thomas
1914–1953

By all odds this Welsh poet was the most distinguished British poet of the mid-century. His play *Under Milk Wood* is generally regarded as his masterpiece. He died in 1953 while on a reading tour of the United States.

Anne Waldman

Along with Ted Berrigan, Waldman was one of the leaders of the "Second Generation." In addition to producing her own voluminous publications, she is also an organizational dynamo. For many years she ran the Poetry Project at St. Mark's-in-the-Bouwerie Church, the primary venue for poetry reading in Greenwich village. for the past decade she has been the prime mover at the Jack Kerouac School of Disembodied Poets at Naropa.

Glenway Wescott
1901–1987

Born in Chicago, Wescott is almost totally unknown today. His first book, a traditional "slender pamphlet of poems" *The Bitterns,* was published in 1920 by his lover, Monroe Wheeler. Wescott went on to win fame and prizes for his novels, especially *The Grandmothers* and *Goodbye.* With the advent of World War II, he gave up fiction and devoted himself to criticism and essays.

Monroe Wheeler
1899–1988

Monroe Wheeler's place in literary history is secure because of his recognition of geniuses and his dedication to helping them get published. He first published Glenway Wescott, as well as Marianne Moore's second pamphlet well before either found a commercial publisher. He also made a lasting contribution to 20th-century culture as one of the founders of The Museum of Modern Art in New York.

John Wieners
1934–

A member of the Black Mountain group and a devoted follower of Charles Olson, Wieners is one of only two poets nominally belonging to this group who actually attended the Black Mountain School. His first book was a slender volume of only twenty-four pages entitled *The Hotel Wentley Poems,* which was published in San Francisco in 1954. His major break-through came about in 1964 with the publication of *Ace of Pentacles.* His flourishing career was sadly brought to an untimely close by a series of nervous breakdowns precipitated by his mother's death.

Marya Zaturenska

A minor poet whose *Cold Morning Sky* won the Pulitzer Prize in 1938. She and her husband Horace Gregory continued to work in literary circles as critics and anthology editors.

Louis Zukovsky
1904–1978

Although Ezra Pound and William Carlos Williams regarded him as a peer, Zukovsky was never widely recognized, yet he continued writing despite critical and popular neglect. Late in life he attracted the attention of several of the younger poets, particularly Creeley and Duncan, who regard-ed him as their mentor after Pound lapsed into silence. Zukovsky published short lyrics, but his life-long preoccupation was with a long, ongoing epic entitled simply *A*.

Titles Published by the Phoenix Book Shop

Bibliographies

A Catalog of Works by Michael McClure, 1956-1965.
  Compiled by Marshall Clements, 1965
A Bibliography of Works by Gregory Corso, 1954-1965.
  Compiled by Robert A. Wilson, 1965
A Bibliography of Works by Charles Olson.
  Compiled by George Butterick and Albert Glover, 1967
A Bibliography of Works by Jack Kerouac, 1939-1967.
  Compiled by Ann Charters, 1967
  Revised Edition, 1976
A Bibliography of Denise Levertov.
  Compiled by Robert A. Wilson, 1972
A Bibliography of Ed Dorn.
  Compiled by David Streeter, 1973
Gertrude Stein: a Bibliography.
  Compiled by Robert A. Wilson, 1974
Gary Snyder: a Bibliography.
  Compiled by Katherine MacNeill, 1985

The Christmas Keepsakes

(all by Robert A. Wilson)

Auden's Library, 1975
Marianne Serves Lunch, 1976
Michael and the Lions, 1980
Rider Haggard's "She", 1977
Tea With Alice, 1978
Faulkner on Fire Island, 1979
Mushrooms, 1981
Six Favorites, 1982
Ten Tintypes and a Tiger, 1983
In the City of Aldus, 1985

The Oblong Octavos

(all limited to 100 numbered and signed and 26
lettered and signed copies,the latter not for sale)

Tipoo's Tiger by Marianne Moore, 1967
(In 1969 a postcard showing the automaton which inspired
this poem was issued by the Victoria and Albert Museum. One
hundred of these cards were laid into a printed folder and sent to
the original purchasers of the pamphlets in 1969.)
Two Songs by W.H. Auden, 1968
Sunrise in Suburbia by John Ashbery, 1968
Complaint by Richard Wilbur, 1968
Three Poems by W.S. Merwin, 1968
The Painter Dreaming in the Scholar's House
  by Howard Nemerov, 1968
Achilles' Song by Robert Duncan, 1969
The Blue Sky by Gary Snyder, 1969
Plane Pomes by Michael McClure, 1969
Youth by John Wieners, 1970
Tlatelolco: a Sequence from Que by Tim Reynolds, 1970

Initial by Louis Zukovsky, 1970
Ankh by Gregory Corso, 1971
New Year Blues by Allen Ginsberg, 1972
Leper's Cry by Peter Orlovsky, 1972
Poem by Elizabeth Bishop, 1973
Yannina by James Merrill, 1973
Loba As Eve by Diane di Prima, 1975
Three Poems by Galway Kinnell, 1976
Am Trak by Amiri Baraka, 1979

Miscellaneous Publications

Ace of Pentacles by John Wieners (cloth, paper, and signed
    limited), 1964
The Under-wood Poems by Jeffrey Kindley (cloth and signed
    limited), 1966
Motor Automatism by Gertrude Stein (paper), 1969
Black Alephs by Jack Hirschman (cloth and paper), 1969
The Night Last Night by Gregory Corso (paper), 1972
The Women Poem by Tim Reynolds (cloth and paper), 1973
Greenwich Village As It Is by Djuna Barnes (cloth), 1978

The Phoenix Guest Book

Naturally, most of my encounters with poets and writers took place in the shop rather than in their homes, since most of them did not live in the Manhattan area. I've recounted in the preceding chapters my memories of those whose homes I visited frequently. The following is a list of all the writers of whatever ilk who visited the Phoenix Book Shop. A few I knew only from correspondence, and they are indicated with an asterisk*. The list may not be totally complete—after all it is now nearly forty years since I walked into 18 Cornelia Street as the owner. To refresh my memory, I've consulted two sources: first of all, checks the Phoenix issued to various writers, and secondly, one of my greatest treasures, a two-volume "guest book" in which I asked the writer-visitors to write something, provided I remembered to ask them to do so.

Helen Adam
Leonie Adams*
Edward Albee
Daisy Aldan
Donald Allen
Michael André
David Antin
Brother Antoninus
 (William Everson)

John Ashbery
W.H. Auden
Amiri Baraka
 (LeRoi Jones)
George Barker*
Julian Beck
Michael Benedikt
Jerry Benjamin
Carol Bergé

Bill Berkson

Danniel Berrrigan

Ted Berrigan

Wendell Berry*

John Berryman*

Elizasbeth Bishop*

Paul Blackburn

Doug Blazek

Roberts Blossom

Robert Bly

Victor Bokris

Louise Bogan

Philip Booth*

George Bowering

Joe Brainard

Ray Bremser

John Malcolm Brinnin*

Joseph Brodsky

William Bronk

Chandler Brossard

James Broughton*

Michael Brownstein

Olive Ann Burns

William Burroughs

Tony Buttita

Reed Bye

Sandy Campbell

Ann Charters

Sam Charters

John Ciardi*

Amy Clampitt

Tom Clark

Andrei Codrescu

Victor Coleman

Tram Combs

Kirby Congdon

Clark Coolidge

Cid Corman

Alfred Corn

Gregory Corso

Jonathan Cott

Douglas Crase

Robert Creeley

Fielding Dawson

Wesley Day

Allen de Loach

Babette Deutsch*

James Dickey*

Ray di Palma

Diane di Prima

Ed Dorn

Ree Dragonette

Martin Duberman

Robert Duncan

Jim Early

Richard Eberhart*

George Economou

Russell Edson*

Larry Eigner*

Richard Elman

Kenward Elmslie

Theodore Enslin

Clayton Eshleman

Larry Fagin

Harry Fainlight

Lawrence Ferlinghetti

Edward Field

Kimball Flaccus

Charles Henri Ford

David Franks

Anne Fremantle

Donald Gallup

Kenneth Gangemi

Isabella Gardner

Jean Garrigue

Barbara Gibbs

Barry Gifford

Alan Ginsberg

Dana Gioia

John Giorno

Andrew Glaze

Emilie Glen

Mitchell Goodman

Edward Gorey

Ted Greenwald

Richard Grossinger

John Guare

Thom Gunn

Brion Gysin

Herman Hagedorn*

Donald Hall

Dan Halpern

Walter Hamady

Marguerite Harris

Dave Haselwood

Boddie Louise Hawkins

Robert Hazel

Seamus Heaney*

Lin Hejinian

Piero Heliczer

David Henderson

William Heyen

Dick Higgins

Jack Hirschman

Daniel Hoffman*

Spencer Holst

Edwin Honig

Katherine Hoskins*

Richard Howard

Barbara Howes

Andrew Hoyem

Will Inman

Christopher Isherwood

Randall Jarrell*

Ted Joans

Ray Johnson

Hettie Jones

Erica Jong

Leandro Katz

Robert Kelly

Jack Kerouac*

John Keys

David Kherdian

Jeff Kindley

Galway Kinnell

Eric Kiviat

Bill Knott

Zan Knudsen

Kenneth Koch

Richard Kostelanetz

Seymour Krim

Stanley Kunitz*

Tuli Kupferberg

Greg Kuzma

Joanne Kyger

Michael Lally

Gerrit Lansing

James Laughlin

Robert LaVigne

Denise Levertov

Philip Levine

Harry Lewis

Ron Loewinsohn

John Logan

Sam Loveman
Lewis MacAdams
Gerard Malanga
Alan Marlowe
Jack Marshall
Harry Mathews
J D McClatchy
Michael McClure
Joseph McElroy
Terrence McNally
Taylor Mead
Eve Merriam
James Merrill
W.S. Merwin
Paul Metcalf
Jack Micheline
Christopher Middleton
Ursule Molinaro
Marianne Moore
Dom Moraes
Brad Morrow
Eric Mottram
Eileen Myles
Howard Nemerov
John Frederic Nims*
Howard Norse
Alice Notley
Charles Olson*
Toby Olson
Joel Oppenheiner
Peter Orlovsky
Maureen Owen
Ron Padgett
Doug Palmer*
Claude Pelieu
S.J. Perelman

Michael Perkins
Stan Persky
Fritz Peters
Robert Peters
Simon Pettit
Felice Picano
Tom Pickard
Charles Plymell
James Purdy
Rochelle Ratner
Tom Raworth
Alistair Reed
Tim Reynolds
Laura Riding
 (Jackson)*
Rene Rickard
Edouard Roditi
Harry Roskolenko
Jerome Rothenberg
Michael Rumaker
Ed Sanders
Aram Saroyan
Dan Saxon
Peter Schjeldahl
Philip Schulze
James Schuyler
Armand Schwerner
Maurice Sendak
David Shapiro
Karl J. Shapiro*
Ron Silliman
Charles Simic
Louis Simpson
Patti Smith
William Jay Smith
Jay Socin

Jean Stafford
William Stafford*
Francis Steegmuller
Gerald Stern
Alan Swallow*
May Swenson
Szabo
Lorenzo Thomas
Ruthven Todd
Tony Towle
Thomas Tranströmer
Quincy Troupe
Gael Turnbull*
Parker Tyler
Tambimutti
John Tytell
Tom Verlaine
Paul Violi
C. Vandenheuvel
Robert Vas Dias
Hunce Voelcker
Andreii Voznesensky*
Peter Veireck*
Diane Wakoski
Anne Waldman
Keith Waldrop
RosmarieWaldrop
Lewis Warsh
Tom Weatherley
Tony Weinberger
James Weill
Glenway Wescott
Philip Whalen*
Nathan Whiting
John Wieners
Richard Wilbur*

Jonathan Williams
Lanford Wilson
William S. Wilson
Donald Windham
Charles Wright*
Andrew Wylie
John Yau
Marguerite Young
Bill Zavatsky
Harriet Zinnes
Louis Zukofsky

This book was designed and set
by Angela Werner
using the typefaces Adobe Garamond and Virile.